HOW
TO
INFLUENCE
PEOPLE

BE YOUR
BEST

HOW TO INFLUENCE PEOPLE

Motivate, Inspire and
Get the Results You Want

CHRIS HELDER

WILEY

First published as *The Ultimate Book of Influence* in 2013 by John Wiley & Sons Australia, Ltd, 42 McDougall St, Milton Qld 4064

Office also in Melbourne

This edition first published in 2019 by John Wiley & Sons Australia, Ltd

Typeset in 12.5/14.5pt Arno Pro

© Helder Consulting Pty Ltd

The moral rights of the author have been asserted

A catalogue record for this book is available from the National Library of Australia

Printed in USA by Quad/Graphics

V008756_022219

Disclaimer

The material in this publication is of the nature of general comment only, and does not represent professional advice. It is not intended to provide specific guidance for particular circumstances and it should not be relied on as the basis for any decision to take action or not take action on any matter which it covers. Readers should obtain professional advice where appropriate before making any such decision. To the maximum extent permitted by law, the author and publisher disclaim all responsibility and liability to any person, arising directly or indirectly from any person taking or not taking action based on the information in this publication.

Contents

Foreword

The business world does not have an information problem! We are one Google click away from a lifetime of information about any topic we can think of. We have more information than we can possibly need, in fact we are drowning in it. What we have is an implementation problem. I see this in the business world every day. We have meetings where people spend an hour saying nothing tangible and everyone walks out and things stay the same. People go to conferences see amazing speakers, have insightful brainstorming sessions, yet go back to work and forget all of it after dealing with 530 emails.

Approximately 76 per cent of all change efforts in organisations fail and 65 per cent of all strategy is never actioned. The reality is people don't implement the things they learn: they just keep following the same behaviour patterns over and over again. Why? Most of the information we receive requires us to break it down and make it relevant and we are simply too busy and tired to do this.

I first saw Chris Helder when he was running a full-day workshop on influence and sales. I was immediately struck by his facilitation skills and masterful use of comedy. However, as I watched him present I was stunned by his ability to take concepts, break them down into first principles so that they became practical and easy to implement. He gave the group a suite of tools that they could walk out of the room and implement the very next day. They didn't need to have more meetings or do more research: they could do it there and then. In fact when I touched base with his client he said that on the Monday morning following the conference he could hear his team use Chris's techniques and they saw immediate results. Anyone can make a concept complicated: a true genius takes something complex and distils it to make it simple.

I was so impressed by his presentation that I asked Chris to personally mentor me on sales and influence. My business was immediately changed and I still use his techniques today. Just quietly, some of them I use at home too (don't tell my wife that). Breaking down the e-wall was a revelation to me and saved my business so much time and effort. 'Sunsets' made me look at my life differently and altered my behaviour, particularly in my personal life. 'Positive, positive, positive — negative' is a technique that I not only use in sales and my presentations, but also in my parenting style.

In this world of inaction, Chris's work is a breath of fresh air. It just works. It is universal and leads to better outcomes. Enjoy this book and marvel at the complexity in his simplicity.

Dr Adam Fraser, author of *The Third Space*

About Chris Helder

Chris Helder is a communication expert and master storyteller whose presentations have radically transformed how thousands of people worldwide communicate with clients, customers, colleagues, family, staff and teams. He has been a professional speaker for 17 years and has given some 2200 presentations around the world.

He is the author of three Wiley best-selling books:

- » *The Ultimate Book of Influence* (2013)
- » *Useful Belief* (2015)
- » *Cut the Noise* (2017)

Chris speaks at conferences in the areas of communication, mindset, human potential, leadership, customer experience and, of course, how to influence other people.

Introduction:
the new reality

Do influence skills matter today?

How important is face-to-face influence in a world of email, text messaging and social media? Clearly influence has changed. But is it still as important as it used to be?

The way that business and sales are done today is without a doubt different from the way it has ever been before. Businesses and brands are embracing the digital age. They are using electronic communications and social media more than ever to promote and sell. We live in a world where decision makers are online and contactable 24 hours a day and seven days a week. Being 'out of the office' means nothing any more, as workers engage in a new era of trying to find balance between work and life.

So why then has the ability to influence a sale or an idea often become harder? Why has the timeline to get a contract signed stretched out for so many businesses? This is primarily due to three reasons:

1. The customer in business today is being protected by what I refer to as the electronic wall or, more simply, the e-wall. As its name suggests, this is a virtual wall

of email and social media behind which your clients can now delay or procrastinate the decision process involved with a sale or a proposal. This, of course, leaves the business development experts unable to use their face-to-face influence skills in order to close the deal.

2. The person presenting the proposal also hides behind the e-wall. It is often easier to just send an email than force the issue to actually create an environment where face-to-face influence can take place. This leads to an extended game of e-pong, which I will explain in the first part of this book. Either way, timeframes for closing deals blow out and often the business is missed simply because there was no leverage created by actually meeting with the decision makers.

3. People are not as good at face-to-face influence skills as they used to be. The pattern of communication has become less about face to face, and it is now acceptable to do business via email. Don't get me wrong — we all need to embrace the digital age. It has provided our world with an unprecedented level of access to communication at the touch of a button. However, face-to-face influence skills have not become redundant. In fact, they are more important than ever if we are to learn how to break down the e-wall.

This book is about influencing people in the new reality. It is about embracing change, and at the same time developing outstanding genuine communication skills. It is about giving you those skills of influence.

The skills in this book do not deny anything that is happening in society today and they adhere to the trends of the new reality. I want to deliver a series of tools to help you come up with solutions to break down some of these new barriers. By starting with the acknowledgement that business methodology is different today, this book will help you tackle the reality. I won't preach a method that does not reflect how sales and influence are done in the real world environment. Your best chance of influencing a decision maker still lies in face-to-face communication.

Often audiences at my presentations are made up of salespeople. They want to increase their ability to influence others, and in the process increase their sales revenue. There are generally two types of salespeople. There are salespeople who *love* being a salesperson. Those people love prospecting, love the thrill of the chase, love presenting their unique selling proposition and love the buzz of closing the sale and collecting commission. If that is you — you are going to love this book. The fact is that I am going to share with you some tools of influence that flat out *work*. Your results are going *up*.

For the second type of salesperson who is interested in influence skills, you have picked up this book for some other reason. You may not see yourself as driven by money or driven by commission. Instead, maybe your role has changed at work in the current economic climate. Suddenly, you are being asked to sell to customers. Perhaps your company has undergone a culture change and they are really driving the bottom line. Perhaps you have had a job change and you are now finding yourself needing to sell something. Maybe this is something you have never really done before and you are looking for some great tips on how to get started. Once again, you will love this book.

This book is loaded with simple tools that will help you meet budget and start down a path of sales and influence that you are comfortable with. At the many sales conferences I speak at, there is always a clear connection between the growth of the business and the ability of the sales team to influence the clients.

Recently, I was presenting at a sales conference in Hawaii. I had finished my talk and I wandered into a sports bar to watch the NBA finals. I sat at the bar and started talking to the man next to me. The conversation started about LeBron James and the level of spice on the buffalo chicken wings we were eating when we began talking business. He was a national sales manager for a global skin care company. He turned to me and asked me a very direct question. 'Chris, you talk at all these conferences. What do you really talk about? Ultimately, what is it that you believe makes a great salesperson?'

My answer came quickly with congruence. 'That's easy,' I said. 'The key is *certainty* and *simplicity*. Great people of influence are certain about what they believe and they are able to present their message in a way that is simple for people to get their head around.'

He smiled. 'That is a great answer. You're right — that's it.'

The reality, however, is there are a great number of salespeople who are what I call PFNs (product-flogging nerds). You can watch the PFNs in action when their idea of selling is to flip through pages of their proposal. They flip from page to page explaining the graphs that demonstrate market share, company information and increased revenue. Actually, I call these salespeople the PTPFNs (page-turning product-flogging nerds).

Many salespeople put their hand up at this point and claim that they used to be one of those people. They tell me how they used to flip pages, but now they have launched into the 21st century and do their presentations on an electronic tablet such as the iPad. One of the first tablet presentations I ever observed with a salesperson flipping pages with their finger and thinking themselves clever completely disengaged the client. The salesperson was failing to look at and connect with their client. Ultimately, they were simply an IPPTPFN (iPad page–turning product-flogging nerd) and they failed to do the one thing that really makes a difference. They failed to influence that client.

Other people might have picked up this book to improve their leadership skills. Perhaps you find yourself having to manage people and bring them together for a common goal. Many people are thrust into roles at work and in life where they are suddenly expected to lead people. This is often a terrifying moment when people are stricken with self-doubt. That is totally normal and, congratulations, you are in the right place! This book will give you an understanding of people that will allow you to manage them more effectively and ultimately influence the people that you work with to achieve the best results.

At the leadership conferences that I speak at, there is always a clear connection between the leader's influence skills and the results of the team. As the saying goes, 'Great organisations grow from the top, and a fish rots from the head.'

You may, however, be an experienced leader who is simply looking for an edge. The tools in this book have helped CEOs and managing directors improve their ability to influence and control outcomes. It is critical that the leadership team is equipped with the tools to lead the team to success. If the leadership team is not willing to work on influencing skills, results go down and staff retention levels plummet. This book will give leaders the tools to identify what is driving each member of the team and provide ideas on how to drive results with each of those team members.

Perhaps for you it is none of those things. You might have picked up this book for reasons that have nothing to do with sales or leadership. You might have picked up this book because you are looking for a way to improve the quality of your life. You are simply aiming to gain clarity about what it is that you want to achieve and how to get started in the process of not only influencing others but also influencing yourself. This is a book that will take you on a very simple and effective journey and help you gain clarity about your goals, turn the anxiety that we all feel into action and influence people to improve your ability to get what you want!

I have had the privilege of giving more than 2300 presentations to audiences in the last 17 years as a professional speaker. I have presented throughout Australia, New Zealand, Asia, Europe and the United States. One of the exciting parts of my job is the variation in the companies that I have worked with. I have spoken at conferences throughout the finance industry, insurance, real estate, mortgage broking, pharmaceutical, software, wine, travel and many more.

Let me ask you a question. If you could improve your ability to influence people, would your business grow? Do you currently hide behind the e-wall? Is it time to increase your face-to-face time and get in front of people to get the results you deserve? Are you a person who simply wants to get your own way more often?

This is a book about how to influence other people. It is time to recognise the appropriate time to utilise technology and the appropriate time to meet face to face. It is also time to make sure that when you do meet in a direct environment that you have the influence skills to get the result that you want.

By the way, I am a firm believer that if things are presented in a simple way, change can happen very quickly. Therefore, I have picked my favourite influence tools that I talk about at conferences and put them together in this book. Some of these tools will help you understand your customers and some will help you understand yourself. In this book there are some language tools that will help you influence others, and some that will help you get through a random Tuesday with greater effectiveness.

I hope you enjoy this book!

Part I
Influencing yourself — action and clarity

The first part of this book is about influencing yourself. When I say that, it is about creating a new level of action to go achieve what it is you are after. The problem, of course, is many people do not have any idea what it is that they are after. So, this part of the book will address these two main concepts — action and clarity

Three tools will be presented in this section of the book:

Tool number 1: breaking down the e-wall

» How to avoid a game of e-pong, where the customer hides behind the e-wall.

» Strategies for creating leverage and moving that customer to taking action.

» How to create a face-to-face environment to influence the customer directly.

Tool number 2: the butterfly

» How to recognise that the number one thing that holds people back is fear.

» How to change anxiety into an action signal.

» How to use that action signal to create successful habits and new results in business and life.

Tool number 3: the sunset

» How to gain clarity about what area of your life you want greatest results in.

» Using the sunset as a tool to uncover the clarity of others.

» How to use that understanding of others to influence them.

CHAPTER 1
Tool number 1: breaking down the e-wall

Clients are busier than they have ever been before. The easiest way for them to decipher and consider your proposal is when it has been in writing and sent via email. In this way, they are the ones who are in the box seat, able to read and consider the proposal in *their* time. They are able to compare your proposal to other written proposals, shift around the priority of the proposal depending on their workload, and all of this without your being able to exert your power of influence.

This is because the digital age has created a virtual electronic wall, the e-wall, which our clients can now hide behind. The pattern of communication has become less about face-to-face interaction, and it is acceptable to do business via email.

The e-pong timeline

This is a typical interaction for a proposal that is emailed in the new reality. It is a game that I call e-pong! You have researched, found your decision maker and sharpened your angle to win the business.

» You make a call. The decision maker is pleased to hear from you, but he or she is busy. They ask you to put your proposal in writing and send it to them for review, *via email* (one week).

» You send your proposal *via email*.

» The decision maker responds that he or she has received your proposal and will review in due course and respond *via email* (two weeks).

» You follow up *via email* in a couple of weeks after hearing nothing back (four weeks).

» Your decision maker is busy and distracted by the day-to-day running of a business. They take four days to respond to your email and say that they are apologetic but will get back to you shortly with a decision after they chat to the relevant people *via email* (five weeks).

» Based on the reply, you are inclined to give the decision maker another week before hassling them again *via email* for an answer.

» You send another email to your decision maker asking if a decision has been made (six weeks).

» Nothing is heard back, and doubts creep in about the priority your proposal is being given.

» You write *via email* one last time stating that you are just wrapping up the quarter or ticking things off your task list and asking once more whether any decision has been made (seven weeks).

» You receive an answer *via email* four days later from your decision maker, thanking you for the hard work you put into the proposal, but unfortunately other priorities have arisen in the company and they are unable to proceed with the business at this time (eight weeks).

Eight weeks of e-pong, with no result. This has all happened because you let the decision maker hide behind their e-wall. In fact, this happened because *you* also hid behind the e-wall! It takes courage to break down the wall and be in a position to influence that customer face to face.

It is simply *easier* to have an email relationship with someone. It is *easier* to send your client a monthly update or a quarterly newsletter and consider that the job is done. Most of all, it is certainly *easier* to try to win a sale by sending the client a proposal and play e-pong. It is much harder to pick up the phone and get face to face with our clients to cut through all of the procrastination and time wasting.

Don't get me wrong. There are times that email is the only option. I realise that. All I am trying to do is challenge you to think about how you can create more face-to-face interactions. What can you do to break down the e-wall?

Changing timelines

Let's take sales, for example. Salespeople talk to me all the time about the difficulty in getting face to face with their clients so they can utilise their skills of influence. They discuss changing trends in technology and adapting to the way business is done. However, the timeline of a sale has barely changed in terms of basic action plan connect points, but the underlying message consistently flowing through is that the amount of time between first contact and closing has significantly increased.

Why has this happened?

It would be easy for salespeople to stand fast, and claim that the e-wall is just another excuse or a trend, and that if you believe in your being personable and having sound communication skills, then nothing should stop you or delay your sales process. My personal favourite excuse dished out by your average motivational speaker is: 'If it's not working, then you must be doing it wrong!' To my way of thinking, this is less than helpful advice, and certainly does not recognise the changing way that business is being conducted in the 21st century. You cannot deny the advances in technology. The statistics tell us that we are more likely to communicate by email or social media than to pick up the phone or meet face to face. We are nearly all capable of conducting business in a completely mobile environment and we are more contactable than ever with our portable devices and Wi-Fi technology, and yet to close a sale is taking longer than ever before.

Five strategies to break down the e-wall

Here are five strategies you can use to help break down the e-wall and stop playing so much e-pong.

1 IDENTIFY THE DECISION MAKERS

At some point, usually before you have the opportunity to meet face to face with the client or send them a proposal, you will have spoken to the client on the telephone to set up everything. One of the biggest mistakes that I see people make is that they send through information without knowing exactly who all the decision makers are. They know the person that they are dealing with, however they have not asked the question in terms of who will *really* be making the call.

Now, I know what some of you are thinking: 'Chris, it doesn't work that way in my business! We can't always get to the decision maker right away.' Okay, fair enough. This book is throwing a whole bunch of spaghetti (ideas) at the refrigerator door. If it sticks, take it. If not, let it fall to the floor. However, in your business, I want you to be clear that the person you are presenting to is *definitely* the person who can get you to the *next level* of your sale.

It happens all the time that people speak to a non-decision maker simply because it was *easier* to send them through the information. Often, you were directed to this person as a gatekeeper. You are spending hours putting together a proposal for your business and this non-decision maker is encouraging you to send it through to them where it really has no chance of getting off the ground.

If you want to make sure that you know who all the decision makers are, here is the *gold*. I've tried this question a lot of different ways and this is the way that will give you the best chance to get this information.

> **Amanda, do you mind if I ask you who,** *apart from yourself,* **is involved in making the final decision about this?**

> **Great! As it takes a considerable amount of time and research for me to put a proposal together, when could we arrange a meeting where everyone would be present to maximise the use of all of our time?**

As simple as that is, so many people ask it the wrong way. I hear people say things like, 'Do you mind me asking: are *you* the decision maker with this?'

This is so close, but it leaves a lot of loopholes because it is so easy for the non–decision maker to say, 'Yes, I am the decision maker.' Then, after you spend two hours putting a proposal together for them, they tell you that they have to run it by the boss or by the HR department. You've wasted your time!

The reasons that they say 'Yes, I am the decision maker' may just be that they are one of the decision makers, and they may not want to bother the boss until they have all the information. It could be that they are putting you off. It may simply be a case of ego. However, when you use the words *'apart from yourself'*, they realise the importance of not wasting everyone's time and it also flatters their ego. By the way, if they won't have the meeting with all of the decision makers present, you *may* have just realised that you were going to be put off anyway!

By using these simple words you have increased your ability to know who will be involved in making the final decision.

Give this a try and increase the impact of your time and effectiveness.

2 DICTATE THE BEST METHOD OF COMMUNICATION

It happens all the time that a client will simply say, 'Email your proposal through and we will have a look at it.' It is *easy* for everyone. The first part of the game of e-pong is underway. The question I would ask you is how often does your client dictate how the communication will work through the pitch and decision process? Do you let your client tell you what the best way to contact them is? Can you dictate how it should work?

Ask yourself these three questions:

» What is their preferred method of communication?

» Is that going to be the best form of communication to get your proposal approved?

» What is your strategy to create an environment where you can communicate in the best possible way to get that proposal approved?

Remember, there are times when you are going to have to email the proposal through because that is the method of communication that the client requires. However, let me challenge you: are you hiding behind the e-wall because it is an *easier* option?

Recently, my manager and I put together a sales training proposal for an internet-based company that was using me monthly in different parts of their business. We had sent through an email proposal on how they could save money by buying my time in bulk. If they locked in 15 sessions for the year, they would be able to use me at a better rate than paying one session at a time.

We were playing some e-pong. The email proposal couldn't get approved until the board meeting. The messages from my manager to the decision maker went unanswered. My manager was becoming frustrated. It was time for a wake-up call. Finally, realising that we were falling into this e-pong trap that I talk about all the time, we answered the three questions:

>> Their preferred method of communication is email.

>> This is *not* going to be the best form of communication to get our proposal approved.

>> The strategy is to get Chris face to face for a 15-minute meeting with the managing director.

That strategy worked. I called the MD directly and explained to him that he was simply paying too much. I got in to see him the next day and we negotiated a deal for the 15 days on the spot. It was time to celebrate because we broke the e-wall!

Once again, there are times when this is not possible. However, in an environment where both salespeople and customers can hide behind a game of e-pong, the question is whether there are other communication methods that would be more effective in getting your proposal approved.

3 MAP OUT YOUR DECISION TIMELINE

Part of breaking down the e-wall is making sure that the client knows your expectations of what is going to happen in this process. Giving a client a deadline ensures they have something to aim for and they won't continually shift the decision because of other priorities.

It is very important in creating a decision timeline that there is either an advantage in making a decision now or, alternatively, a disadvantage in delaying the decision. If you have not created any leverage for the client to make a quick decision, it is even easier for the client to hide behind the e-wall. There is no reason for them to do anything. They can sit on your proposal and wait while you become more anxious. I will explore this further in the next part of this book in the pain–pleasure principle.

Ask yourself these questions:

» When do you want the decision to be made?

» What is the advantage for them in making a decision before this deadline?

» What is their disadvantage if they do not make a decision before this deadline?

» Will getting face to face expedite the decision-making process?

Sometimes this process will be out of your control. The question, however, is whether you have mapped out an expectation for the client to make a decision.

You need to make sure that you put forward a reason for the client to make a decision in an appropriate timeframe. Otherwise, there is no reason for them to prioritise you. Some examples of this may include:

» In the speaking industry, the client has to make a decision to lock in the date because otherwise the speaker may no longer be available.

» In the real estate industry, the buyer has to make a decision to offer now because if they wait for Saturday afternoon, after the open house, there may be a new buyer who is interested in offering as well. This will create competition and drive up the price.

» In the landscaping industry, the client has to make a decision to get started with the project now if they want to have their pool in by the summer holidays.

By the same token, make sure that, at the end of every communication, you begin putting into practice a habit that I call next steps. In the decision timeline, what do you want the next step in the process to be?

Tip

Here's how to get to next steps by email:

> 'The next step would be for me to meet all the decision makers face to face and present the proposal. Is there a time that all the decision makers come together and I would be able to meet them?'

Here's how to get to next steps by phone:

> 'After you've had a chance to read the proposal, the next step would be for us to meet again next week to look at moving forward. What time will suit you next week?'

To execute this most effectively, it is important to nail the client down for the next steps while you have them on the line and while their interest is still piqued.

4 LEAVE SOMETHING IN THE CHAMBER

Without underselling your product or service, can you get the client's attention in the written proposal, but leave some information out which is best presented face to face?

People frequently put their heart and soul into their proposal and then leave no other reason to actually meet the client face to face. The customer then has all the power and can very easily email and say, 'I have all the information. I will read through it and get back to you.'

What is unique about your product or service that would drive the *need* for a face-to-face meeting with all the decision makers? Is there something that you can leave up your sleeve that would be particularly compelling to your customer? For example, a salesperson may ask for a 30-minute meeting and explain that if the client will meet with them, there will be something that can be *added* for them in the negotiation. This could be things like:

» free delivery

» extra services

» priority customer service

» benefits

» better price.

This will give you more power in closing. If you have additional information ready to pull out, you can use it at a critical point in the presentation or negotiation.

5 CAST OFF DEAD WOOD

It is important to back yourself to stick to the decision timeline deadlines. Let me ask you a question. How much time do you waste by chasing business that will never happen? Sometimes it takes nerves of steel, but it is important to maintain your value and credibility in the marketplace. There are times it is better to recognise are you better off chasing a new client than someone who is only going to waste your time.

I come across this at conferences where an organisation will say to me that their salespeople are great at having conversations, but are not getting the deals done. Remember, there is a big difference between a great conversationalist and a great salesperson! The great salespeople are good at recognising that long conversations or extended e-pong is simply going nowhere. There is a time and a place to cut the cord.

Chapter 1 summary

The new reality is that the majority of people would rather communicate via email, text message and social media than face to face. We all have the ability to communicate with more people in less time than ever before. That has made the world an exciting, smaller place, and information accessible and virtually instant.

That being said, there is a growing frustration as customers are often playing a game of e-pong and hiding behind the e-wall. This means that while it is easier to get them the information, in some ways it is harder for you to get them to make a decision. I challenge you to make a conscious effort to workshop what needs to happen in your business to break the e-wall and create more direct communication opportunities which lead to greater results.

Quick questions

» Can you do a better job at finding out who all the decision makers are?

» Are you consistent at discovering preferred methods of communication with your customers?

» If so, is the client's preferred method also the most effective?

» Do you lay out a decision timeline with your customers and establish clear expectations?

» Are you in the habit of laying out Next Steps at every contact point in the decision cycle with your clients?

» Do you leave something in the chamber for face-to-face meetings? Do you leave clients with a reason to need to meet with you?

» Are some customers simply wasting your time? Are there clients in your business that are simply taking too much time for no reward?

The digital age has **created** a virtual electronic wall, **the e-wall**, which our clients can now hide behind.

———————————

CHAPTER 2
Tool number 2: the butterfly

The number one thing that holds people back is fear.

This fear is perfectly normal. It usually manifests itself in the pit of your stomach where you feel a flutter of anxiety. It is a feeling that comes from the thought of picking up the phone or getting face to face with the client. It is so much easier if you don't do these things. The fact of the matter is that the feeling goes away when you decide to email the proposal instead of presenting it. There is no direct rejection with email. For most people, an email rejection means that the client rejected the idea. Face-to-face rejection means they rejected you as a person.

So it is a lot easier to hide behind the e-wall. In fact, it is a lot easier to procrastinate or avoid the action that needs to be taken to be successful.

This flutter of anxiety shows up in many different scenarios. It could be any of these words that people say to themselves that create this anxiety:

» 'I should pick up the phone and set up an appointment to go and *see* this client. I know I should do it. I don't know — it's just easier to email them this information.'

» 'I should call the company and enquire about this new position. I should do it. I don't know — I will probably just email them my CV. It's easier to email it.'

» 'I should go to that audition. I should go. I don't know — I probably don't have a chance at it anyway. Maybe I'll skip it.'

» 'I should call that person. I should call her or him. I don't know — I doubt they would want to go to the concert with me anyway. I won't call them. If I run into them somewhere else, well, it will be meant to be.'

» 'I should go to the gym. I should go. I said I was going to go after work. I don't know — I am tired. I feel like sitting down and watching television. I won't go. I'll stay home. I'll start Monday.'

In all of those cases, fear was the driver that stopped these people from achieving what they wanted. The fear held them back from taking a chance and moving forward towards realising their outcome. Also, in all of those cases, the fear manifested itself as a feeling in the pit of their stomach. It felt like anxiety, which often immobilises a person and stops them taking action. Instead, that feeling of anxiety freezes people. It is very common that people procrastinate and put off what it is that they need to do.

Everyone has had a time when they put off something that they should be doing — phone calls to make, meetings to attend, opportunities to follow up, even just paying a bill. Everyone has had the experience of procrastination.

The emotion that follows is guilt. People feel guilty for not making the calls they were supposed to make. They feel guilty for not doing the paperwork they should have done. They feel guilty for not going to the gym as they promised themselves. And, ultimately, with the e-wall they feel guilty for not picking up the phone and trying to make a face-to-face appointment.

Most people believe then that guilty people would become apologetic. Instead, a funny thing happens. When people feel guilty, their natural defence mechanism is to move into a defensive, negative state.

Imagine a scenario where the salesperson failed to make the appropriate number of phone calls. They did send off a series of proposals to customers and they were waiting to hear back from all of them. However, deep down they knew they should have been following those proposals up with phone calls and face-to-face meetings. Instead, they played some e-pong and were frustrated that they were not getting the go-ahead.

Because they were avoiding making the phone calls, they felt guilty. Because they felt guilty, they moved into a negative, defensive state of mind. They began to blame the customers. They started to question the product. They started to gossip with co-workers about the lack of leadership in the department. Ultimately, they started to become a toxic worker in the office. This is all due to procrastination and a lack of action. This is due to the fact that hiding behind the e-wall creates an incredible amount of frustration for the salesperson because they are not getting the responses they want.

The fear has led to a downward trajectory that will ultimately lead to an environment where they will either quit or be asked to leave.

What if we could change all this? What if we could turn this anxiety into something positive and change this process for people forever?

Let's do it!

Avoidance and how it works

The typical structure of avoidance works in the way shown in figure 2.1 (overleaf).

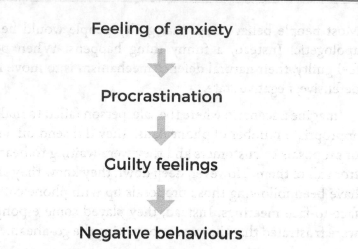

Feeling of anxiety

Procrastination

Guilty feelings

Negative behaviours

Figure 2.1: the structure of avoidance

Let's take exercise as a lighter example about how avoidance may work. Imagine you are trying on clothes in one of those department stores where there is a mirror and some bad lighting. In fact, imagine it is one of those dressing rooms that has six mirrors and when you walk in you can see yourself from every possible angle. Then, while trying on clothes, you have that moment of standing there in your underwear looking at your body from six different angles.

There are always a few people in the audience that would think, 'Fantastic! I'm really loving the way my body looks!' However, most people would probably feel some sense of anxiety. They would have that feeling of anxiety in the pit of their stomach because they know it is time to do something to improve their fitness.

What happens at this point is that a few people might walk out of that dressing room and make a plan to get fit. They know it is time and they are going to get started!

But that is not most people. Most people would think that they needed to do something. However, even though they have the best of intentions, they will get busy over the course of the rest of the day. When they do, they will find a reason not to go to the gym. They will procrastinate over going and this will lead to a powerful feeling of guilt.

I have had women tell me about how they do this when they are at work and plan to go to the gym at the end of the day. Then, during their work day, they serve cake to everyone for Sarah's birthday. It would be rude not to eat the cake! So, having eaten cake, they put off going to the gym. However, it gets worse. They already feel guilty as they go home and sit on the couch, and then they decide to pick up a magazine. There are photos of beautifully dressed actresses and supermodels clad in the best designer fashions. Suddenly, the woman begins to *talk* to her magazine. 'Whatever, Blake Lively! I'd look like that too if all I had to do all day is work out!'

This has moved her into a negative state of mind. Moments later her husband walks in the door. The man, not always the smartest creature on the planet, says the worst thing possible as he enters the room. 'Oh, you're home. I didn't think you were going to be here. I thought you were going to the gym.' (More guilt.)

'What are you saying? Are you saying I'm fat?' (Negative behaviours.)

Human beings do this all the time — we snap at other people simply because we feel guilty about our lack of action in spite of our good intention.

Salespeople have this happen all the time. They get the anxiety of knowing they are supposed to make some long-term prospecting phone calls. They even schedule their prospecting time for Wednesday afternoon between two and four. Then some other stuff comes up and they decide to put off making the phone calls. It is easy to do this, because the prospecting and following up proposals with phone calls is not urgent. At the same time, deep down they know their business is heading along a negative trajectory due to this lack of discipline in client contact. And this leads to a level of guilt for the salesperson. They know they should be making more phone calls, creating more meetings and doing more pro-active business-building activity. Instead they are hiding behind the e-wall. They have an idea: 'I'll just send out an e-newsletter instead.'

Eventually, when the boss pulls them aside to discuss their lack of results, the salesperson responds in a negative and defensive way. They begin to blame the boss, clients, market, office and even co-workers to justify their behaviour. This is not useful.

Do you interpret that little feeling in the pit of your stomach as a *positive* or *negative* experience? Most people say that this is a negative experience.

Never again.

Paying attention to action signals

From now on, I want you to change that experience forever. Imagine if you changed the perception of that experience to something positive instead of something negative. Normally, the words that people associate with that feeling are words like anxiety and fear. Those are incredibly negative associations. What if you could change that?

In fact, the feeling that you get in your stomach is a gift from your body. It is an *action signal*. It is your body's way of telling you to *do* something. It is trying to get your attention. It is completely *positive*.

What if the flutter in your stomach was not anxiety. Instead, what if it was something beautiful? What if it was a butterfly? The butterfly is the messenger. The butterfly is coming to help you. It is your inner voice trying to steer you in the right direction. It is telling you to do something. The butterfly is telling you to take action in a positive way to make your work and life better than it is.

Let's take the exercise example again. If the butterfly appears as you survey your body from six uninspiring angles, your inner voice is telling you that it is time to get healthy. If the butterfly is an action signal then the process would look like figure 2.2.

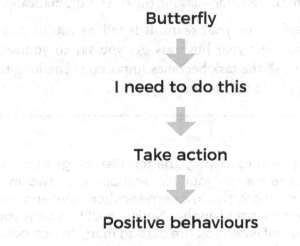

Figure 2.2: the butterfly as an action signal

The most important words you say all day are the words you say to yourself, about yourself, when you are alone. Imagine if the words you say to yourself when you feel the butterfly and have identified why your body is sending you a message are these words:

I need to do this!

Suddenly, the feeling that was negative and felt like anxiety is now a gift from your body serving as an action signal. Your response is 'I need to do this' and so you take action.

Let's tie this back to the e-wall. Most people know when they should get face to face to present a proposal. But it is just so much easier to email it. But if you listen to the butterfly and decide that this is a situation where you need to get face to face, you can overcome the anxiety and set up the meeting. You need to do this. You need to take action. The result is positive and you can cut down the decision-making timeframe dramatically.

The butterfly is on your team. It is telling you to pick up the phone to grow your business. As you say to yourself, 'I need to do this!' the task becomes important. The long-term prospecting phone calls become a *priority*.

Tip

I challenge you to identify the top five things that you procrastinate over in your life. Perhaps pick two in a work environment, two in a home environment and one relating to health and energy. Notice what language you use to yourself when you are getting ready to postpone those activities. Is that language useful and getting you closer to what you want or is it taking you further away from your outcome?

I challenge you to notice how the process of taking action changes when you simply say to yourself, 'I need to do this! My body is telling me to take action!' When it becomes a positive instead of a negative, you are grateful that your body spoke to you. The beautiful butterfly got you moving!

My best advice is simply pick up the phone! The first call is the hardest. Once you get into a flow, the calls become easier and easier. You are taking action. Two hours of good conversation with potential clients can lead you to getting in the car and driving home feeling a sense of accomplishment. You know you have done everything possible to break down the e-wall.

Chapter 2 summary

All the time people avoid tasks that should be prioritised. I challenge you to identify the activities in your life that you should do more of and take action to achieve those tasks. Be aware of what your body is telling you. In the past, your interpretation of the feelings in the pit of your stomach may have been negative. You may have interpreted those feelings using a negative word like anxiety.

Instead, I challenge you to flip that. Think of the feeling as the butterfly effect. It is your body's way of communicating with you in a positive way to encourage you to take action to accomplish something that you need to prioritise. The completion of that task will give you a sense of achievement and in doing so will give you a sense of control over your business and your life. The first part of being influential is influencing yourself.

Quick questions

» What activities do you procrastinate on that you know should be prioritised?

» Do you catch yourself falling into a negative state when you have failed to prioritise and take action on important tasks?

» How can you change your own language with yourself when you feel the butterfly effect?

» In which areas of your business and life will you be able to apply the butterfly effect?

It is a lot easier to **procrastinate** or avoid the action that needs to be **successful**.

_____

CHAPTER 3
Tool number 3: the sunset

Breaking down the e-wall has everything to do with having a desire to *actually* break down the e-wall. Many people take the easy option because they simply don't want their job to be challenging. Why do it harder if it's not what you really want to do?

But people who influence are *certain*. In order to be certain about anything, there has to be a clarity about what it is that you are really trying to achieve. When there is certainty, breaking down this e-wall and wanting to influence people happens more naturally.

This part of the book is designed to challenge you to think about what it is you are *really* trying to achieve in your life. My goal is to get you to think about how you can create a perfect world scenario. I am positive that achieving that perfect world scenario will happen only through a lot of dedication and hard work. There are no real short cuts. There is a direct correlation between success and the level of hunger to achieve your dreams. I want to challenge you to increase your desire to hit your vision. But a lot of people are not sure what that really means for them. What does that perfect world scenario really look like?

An old Buddhist proverb says, 'When the student is ready, the teacher will appear.' Opportunities for success are often missed simply because the individual is not ready for that success. A select few seem to have been born ready for success, but for most people there is a catalyst that drives them to be hungry to achieve it. That could be anything from getting married, having children, wanting a promotion, setting a financial goal or simply deciding to create a better lifestyle.

Let's go to the big picture. The first part of this book is about influencing yourself. It's tough to do that if you've fallen so far down the rabbit hole that you can't see what it is that you are really trying to achieve.

I love doing conferences in California and Western Australia because I love going to the beach in those places and watching the sun set over the ocean. It is a magical time of day. The sun lowers itself slowly over the water until there is just a bit left and it sends glowing orange light over the water. Then, suddenly, it goes poof!, and disappears. Just like that. You would think it would take a really long time for the sun to finally disappear, but it doesn't. It signifies for me the end of the day. It's a good moment of clarity for me every day. I can look back on that day and think about what I did well and what I did not do well. There is truth in the end-of-the-day looking back.

Using the sunset

The great thing is that we don't actually need to go to the beach to do this. We can create a sunset for ourselves by creating a perfect world scenario for the future. The sunset is a metaphor for the future.

The sunset is a powerful tool around timeline mastery. It is a tool to help you master your timeline and gain great clarity about what it is you want to achieve over the next two months, the next six months, the next 12 months or the next 55 years. What is your two-month sunset? What is your six-month sunset? Your 12-month sunset? Your 55-year sunset? Working out your sunset is the best way of gaining clarity in any situation.

The sunset is a tool for creating hunger. One of greatest complaints that I get from sales managers and directors is that they want more hungry salespeople. The sales managers are frustrated because they have salespeople who have tremendous potential, but they don't want to do the extra that will get the deal over the line. Many sales managers are frustrated that they don't have salespeople who are hungry enough to do the prospecting and make the number of phone calls that they need to in order to be successful.

Often the lack of hunger comes from a lack of clarity. As I like to say, 'He or she that shoots at nothing generally hits it!'

Let me ask you a question. Have you ever felt like a day goes by, or a week or a month, and the next thing you know six months has gone by and you're not actually sure if you are on target for what you wanted to achieve? Are you actually moving towards where it is you want to get to?

The problem for a lot of people is that they try to set goals by living in the moment. A lot of people out there in the wide world of life are actually living and working and surviving on what I call the hamster wheel of life. Now, on the hamster wheel of life — and if you can picture a hamster on a hamster wheel in your mind right now — that hamster is going around and working hard. They are getting up every day and working hard running around and around inside that hamster wheel. At the end of the day, they are tired, but they are not actually getting anywhere near where it is that they want to get in their life, in the level of accomplishment they want to achieve and, often, they aren't even sure they are running on the right hamster wheel.

The problem is that they are just reacting to what happens in the present.

Getting off the hamster wheel

To illustrate this habit of reacting to the present, I want to set up a timeline (see figure 3.1).

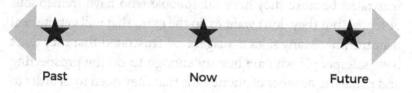

Figure 3.1: timeline

With this timeline, it is critical to understand a few key concepts:

» The truth is in the future (sunset).

» Fulfilment comes from living in the now.

» The past can hold you back.

I want to challenge you in the next part of this book to think about how this timeline applies to your life. In all aspects of your life, I want you to really think about the clarity you have about what it is that you are trying to achieve.

The truth is in the future (sunset)

To make the concept of the sunset come alive, I'm going to use a relationship example. At some of the goal-setting conferences I speak at, I ask all the married men in the room to raise their hand and I challenge them to go home and ask a simple question.

'When you all get home tonight,' I say to them, 'I want you to pour a glass of wine with your wife and ask her a very simple question. Sit down, look her in the eye and ask her, "How do you think our relationship is going at the moment?"'

The audiences always laugh when the married men groan.

'I'm serious,' I continue. 'I want you to sit down and look your wife in the eyes and ask this very simple question. "How do you think our relationship is going at the moment?"'

The answer, I tell them, will often be something like this. She may stir in her seat and then follow with, 'You really want to know? Umm — it's good. I mean — yeah, it's umm, good. I mean I wish we had more time. I wish we had more time together. Actually that's not true. I really wish I had more time for *myself*. It's busy, you know. Now that I think about it. You know what? It's fine.' She says this shaking her head from side to side. 'It's fine. It is. I think it's fine.'

There is no truth in *fine*. Fine is something people use all the time to avoid looking at the truth. How's business? *Fine*. How's your relationship? It's *fine*. How's your body? It's *fine*. I'm too busy at the moment to work on it. There is no truth in the word fine.

In fact, if you wanted to know the truth, you'd ask you wife a question in the future. You would ask her a sunset question. You'd ask her about her three-month sunset.

'Sweetheart,' you'd say, 'let's travel three months from right now [three-month sunset] and imagine that you pick up the phone and you ring your best friend in the world. When you pick up that phone to ring that best friend in three months' time you say these words, "I've never been happier in my relationship than I am right now." For you to say those words, what happened? What's changed? What did I do? What did you do? What did we do together?'

And, gentlemen, you hope she doesn't say, 'For me to say those words I live with the *pool guy* now!'

Either way, that would be the truth.

For you, imagine a three-month sunset from right now. Imagine picking up the phone in three months' time, calling a friend and saying, 'I've never been happier in my job than I am right now. I've never been more connected to my business than I am right now.' For you to say those words, what happened? What did you do? What did you put in place? The answer is the *criteria* you need to action.

Let's go 12 months from right now. Imagine a 12-month sunset — for you to walk in this room 12 months from now and have the body you want to have, for you to feel better physically about how you look, about how you're connected to yourself and your presence. For you to feel that way, what happened? What did you change? The answer is the *criteria* you need to action.

For you to go 18 months from right now and for you to have had the most successful business 18 months of your entire life, what happened? For you to walk in and say to me, 'Chris, I feel better personally and professionally than I've ever felt.' For you to say those words, what happened? What changed for you? For you to get to that sunset, what did you put into place? The answer is the *criteria* you need to action.

It's no different with a long-term sunset. Most people are going through their lives spinning on that hamster wheel. Let me give you the 85-year-old sunset. The 85-year-old sunset is a picture of you, sitting in a chair at 85 years old looking back on the last 20, 30, 40, 50, 60, 70 years of your life. Imagine that you are looking back on the events of your life. Imagine you are sitting in your favourite chair and sipping a glass of wine in front of your open fire and reflecting on everything that has happened. For you to look back on that last period of time, and for you to say to yourself, 'I nailed it. This is exactly what I wanted to do. I lived my life the way I wanted to live my life. I'm thrilled.' For you to feel that way about your life, what happened for you? What did you do? What risks did you take?

The answers about what risks to take lie in the sunset. The criteria for what we need to action and what we need to change lie in the sunset. Many people get to their 85-year-old sunset and realise that they have lived a life of tremendous regret. For you to feel relief instead of regret, what did you do? The answer is the *criteria* you need to action.

When you speak with older people they typically do not regret the things they *did*, but instead regret things that they *didn't* do.

Let's back it all the way up and ask about today. What is your today sunset. I mean, for you to walk into your house at the end of today and say:

> **Wow, great day! I made the most of it.**

For you to say that at the end of today, what happened? The answer is the *criteria* you need to action.

Sunset questions as a selling tool

For salespeople, one of the great uses for the sunset concept is to ask prospective clients sunset questions. These are questions that give clarity about what the gaps are that prevent them moving forward and how they may be able to come up with a solution for these gaps.

An example of a sunset question to ask in my industry, if I sat down with a sales director, would be, 'Twelve months from right now, for you to walk in here and say this was the best year ever, what happened and what changed?'

The answer will include discussion about members of the sales team increasing their selling skills and time management, and creating better habits. Those answers will lead me closer to a sale as I would tailor my sales presentation to have solutions around selling skills, time management and creating winning habits.

What are some examples of sunset questions in your industry? The basic formula for asking these sunset questions would be:

1. Pick a timeframe (for example, 12-month sunset) and ask the client to share what would be their perfect world scenario at the end of that timeframe.

2. Ask and determine what changes would need to happen for that to occur.

The answers will give you criteria to action. Link your sales presentation to how you can help the client take action with those criteria.

A simple example of using sunset questions could be exercise at the gym:

1. Twelve months from now, for you to walk in here and feel good about your body, what would change? What would you be able to do that you cannot do at the moment? What would your body look like?

2. What changes in workout and diet would have to happen to achieve that goal?

The answers to those two questions give you the criteria, so it's time to come up with an action plan!

Interviews and performance reviews

The sunset questions are also very powerful in both interviews and performance reviews.

In an interview environment, asking a sunset question will give you clarity about where someone sees themselves going within your organisation. For example, if you ask a potential employee, 'Twelve months from now, for this to have been the most fulfilling job you've had, what sort of things would have taken place for you?'

The answers might include, 'One of the reasons that I was interested in interviewing for this position was because of the long-term potential. I would love to eventually move into the marketing side of this business and make a career after I've proven myself.'

That is a lot different than if they look at you with a blank stare and mumble, 'Umm, I guess that I would have been paid.'

I would be very hesitant to hire someone who did not have at least a level of clarity about the role, the organisation and what they would like to achieve moving forward.

The performance review is exactly the same. Imagine meeting with a frustrated employee and asking a sunset question. 'I know you have been frustrated over the last 12 months, but let's look at next year. For you to walk in here for your review in 12 months' time and say to me, "This has been the best year for me professionally" what would have happened for you? What will have changed for you?'

Tip

Get clarity with holidays! When people go on holidays, one person often ends up not getting to do everything they wanted. They come home disappointed because there was an activity that they had their heart set on doing, but missed out on.

To make sure this doesn't happen, try using the sunset questions when you are organising your next holiday. Imagine organising your romantic holiday to Bali: 'Honey, for you to get to the end of the holiday and feel you did everything you wanted to do and have this be the best holiday ever, what did we do?' Your partner is likely to respond with something like, 'Well, I definitely want to go snorkelling, do some hiking and I really want to make sure I have three or four days where I just lie on the beach and do nothing.' You've got your criteria: plan away! Have the time of your life!

Fulfilment comes from living in the now

In the past I've had people misunderstand the concept of the sunset and say things like, 'Chris, if you spend all your time worried about the future, you would miss living in the moment.' They'd be right if you didn't look at the *entire* timeline (see p. 108).

The truth is in the future in terms of the *criteria* that we need to action. The criteria that need to be put into action are discovered from gaining the clarity by creating a perfect world scenario. However, the actual living of life, once you've captured a glimpse of that clarity in the future, is in the *moment*. Fulfilment comes from living in the *now*.

I learned a lot about living in the now at the Finding Nemo Submarine Ride at Disneyland. I was doing a conference in Palm Springs, California, and I took my then five-year-old,

Billy the Kid, on the big journey from Australia to California. I thought it would be the perfect opportunity to spend some quality one-on-one time with him and take him to Disneyland. By the way, any parent that gets an opportunity to spend 10 days one-on-one with one of their children shouldn't pass it up. The bond created is phenomenal.

Anyway, there we were at Disneyland and I'm selling the day to him. All morning long, I'm telling him after every ride how good this day is. I'm hearing myself telling him things like, 'How lucky are you buddy to see the real Mickey? How great is that? That's the real Lightning McQueen! Billy, how good was that ice-cream? How good was that water ride?' I was selling the day so hard that I hadn't realised something incredibly important. I was so busy selling the day that I was *missing* it.

There we were about to put our eyes into the periscope on the Finding Nemo Submarine Ride, when I was selling him how good it was going to be. 'Billy, we are going to see Nemo! We are going to see Bruce the Shark! We'll see Dory and Crush the turtle...'

Suddenly come pearls of wisdom as Billy put his hand in the air and stopped me from continuing and said, 'We'll see what we see.'

And with that he put his eyes to the periscope.

> **We'll see what we see.**

That's awesome.

Imagine how *present* you would be on the everyday journey if you approached it to see what you see. Imagine the change in expectations and disappointments. Instead, everything would be happening in front of you and the day would be spent learning on that journey. Not a day has gone by since that I haven't thought about that. As long as the sunset is providing us clarity and guidance, it is critical that we experience the day.

The past will hold you back

I'm always fascinated by the concept of sliding door moments: it has always fascinated me that life can totally change in one moment, or with one decision or even one circumstance. Make a different choice and life would be altered forever.

What comes with that is that there is an entire society of people out there who have made choices in their life that they regret. These moments of regret about the choices they have made often create chips on their shoulders.

Everyone has them to some degree. Some people have many regrets, and they are suffocating future success and possibility. Other people have fewer regrets and don't hold on to emotions like guilt and insecurity as tightly as others.

These regrets are the decisions you made that created chips on the shoulder. For some, they were decisions about what to study, who to marry, whether or not to have children, a profession, moving away from family and friends — the list goes on and on. Many of those decisions people would tell me were 'The best things they ever did!' Others would tell you their story of moments, decisions and circumstances with tremendous regret.

Often, the choices are not ours to make. Everyone can tell you circumstances that were thrust upon them in millions of forms. They are the things you had no control over. They are the things that people said to you or that people did to you; the people that decided not to love you or the people that left you by passing away.

All of these moments, decisions and circumstances are critical in defining the chips that each person carries with them. The more time people play in the arena of the regrets about the past, the harder it is to gain clarity in the sunset or live in the now. Instead, those people live their lives focused on past events that they have no ability to change. It is virtually impossible to influence others until you can master your own timeline. To do that, the chips need to transform themselves from regrets to learning.

Exercise

Whenever an event or something significant has happened in your life, especially if it was somewhat soul destroying, ask yourself two simple questions:

1. Why do you think this happened?

2. What did you learn?

Those two questions can take any significant negative event or chip in your life and turn it into learning. When these questions are asked, your brain can't help but search for a positive response about why that certain event took place and what you learned.

I challenge you, with each of the chips that you have due to moments, decisions and circumstances, to ask yourself those two questions. Because it is an incredible thing when you feel the chips lift off your shoulder and, instead of weighing you down, they make you stronger.

Many people live much of their lives in the negative past. Be very careful to use the past as a series of lessons and not get sucked into the woulda, coulda, shoulda. Turn the negative past into learning and the past will no longer hold you back. Instead, it will serve as a guide, moving towards the sunset and also to making better decisions in the now.

I have had the opportunity to meet so many amazing people. Every so often, I meet someone who possesses a quality that I like to think of as non-anxious presence. This has happened at a conference or a party where I met someone who I just felt was so in control of themselves. They were seemingly better than everyone else. They were truly present and completely comfortable in their own skin. They were just really good at being *themselves*.

I have always wondered what separates that person from so many people who seem self-conscious and anxious. I've worked it out: they are good with their timeline. They are free from the past (turning regrets into learning) and they are clear about the future (clarity). Because they are so good with where they have been and where they are going, they are able to *be* in the moment. They are able to be present and non-anxious. They possess this quality of non-anxious presence.

Show me an anxious leader and I will show you an anxious team. Show me an anxious schoolteacher and I will show you an anxious classroom. Show me an anxious world leader and I will show you an anxious society. Show me an anxious salesperson and I will show you an anxious client.

The land in-between

It was amazing working with people through the global financial crisis and helping them develop strategies for a new financial reality. What I discovered is that in the years between 2009 and 2012 there were a lot of people that were paralysed by their current situation. They had entered a place that I like to think of as a land in-between. What do I mean by this?

This land in-between is a place where everything that has become normal is interrupted. Often, the land in-between comes with a conversation that drops into our lives like an exploding bomb:

- » 'The stock market has crashed.'
- » 'Your position at the company has been eliminated.'
- » 'There has been an accident.'

> » 'The tumour is malignant.'
>
> » 'I don't love you any more.'
>
> » 'Your mother and I are getting a divorce.'
>
> » 'The fertility tests were inconclusive.'

Suddenly the person's life as they know it will never be the same. They are hurled into the land of financial insecurity. They tumble into the world of the unemployed. They find themselves thrown into the land of the suddenly single. Suddenly the person is in this place 'in-between' and they are not sure of the road to a new place of security, hope and normality.

I had an experience in September 2011 that launched me into the land in-between.

The phone call came like out of a movie. It was 4.30 in the morning and I was in a daze as I picked up the receiver. Even in a fog, I could sense the sadness on the other end of the phone from my stepmother.

'Chris, it's Sandy. I have some bad news. Your dad just died.'

It had been a call that I had thought about. He was 69 years old and in total he had suffered four heart attacks over the last 11 years. The real frustration was that I didn't expect that call now. He had just had a hip replacement. The hospital had sent him home, so I assumed he was going to be okay. He was going to have a renewed sense of energy with that new hip.

My father wasn't ready to die. Some people are. My father was still working and, in many ways, doing his best work. At 69, he had found a peace that I believe had eluded him throughout much of my childhood. He was full of plans and goals for the next 10 years.

My dad was very much about the journey of life. What made him remarkable was not his infallibility. It was his humanity. He had learned from his journey. He had learned from many of his mistakes. My dad was about growth. I believe he was a very different man at 69 than he was at 59.

Naturally, I spent a period of time following the death of my father living here. Life as I knew it would never be exactly the same. The phone call had put me into the land in-between, Sadly, one chapter of my life was closed. However, I realised soon afterward that this new chapter of my life without my father had begun. While there will always be a sense of tremendous loss, I realised it was time to move *forward* and *accept* what had happened. It was time to begin living in this new chapter in the book of my life and accept a new reality.

That being said, it never ceases to amaze me how many people live in a state of paralysis in the land in-between. How many people are looking at their industries and realising that life the way they have known it will now be different? They discover that the way they have always done business has changed. What they did in the past is no longer working! However, they are happy to tell you about it every day. They constantly say things like:

'Man, it was easier to sell this stuff 10 years ago. They were good days.'

'The economy is terrible now. This job is no fun any more. I loved it early in my career. They were good days.'

Life is so expensive today. When I was a kid it was easier for parents to raise children.

The truth is that life changes. The things that people did to be successful in the past may not be the things that they have to do to be successful in the future. My father has passed on. I can remember the lessons and the memories of the past. I can cherish the hugs and the times looking up to see him watching me from the sideline. I can hold that close to my heart. However, healing comes when you move *forward*.

It is about using the lessons that were given to me to make a better future. It is also about my trying to be a better man 10 years from now than I am today.

It is no different in business. The fact of the matter is that the past is gone. That chapter is closed. The reality for many people is that the way that they did business a number of years ago may not work today. The activities that they did in the past may not generate business and customer loyalty the way they did before.

Therefore, people have some options. They can look at their current situation and ask themselves what they want to do for the future:

» Idealise the past and wish it was still like it used to be.

» Wallow around in the current land in-between and not take action to change, but rather continue to do the things that are not working as effectively any more.

» Accept a new reality!

The new reality can be exciting. The challenge of the journey is exciting. It is not about being infallible. Instead, it is the opposite. I challenge you to take the steps into the new reality for your business. What are the things that you need to put into action? Twelve months from now, for you to walk up to me at a conference and say, 'Chris, this has been the best year of my life — professionally, physically and in terms of my relationship. I have never been happier than I am today.' For you to say those words, what did you start doing? What did you stop doing? I challenge you to find the clarity that will give you the ability to influence yourself.

Chapter 3 summary

The reason that I started this book with influencing yourself and getting good with your timeline is that it is impossible to truly influence other people unless you are able to have those two magic words — certainty and simplicity. Once you have a level of certainty about your timeline, people will listen to what it is that you have to say. It is very difficult to truly influence people if you are unclear and do not know what it is that your sunset is all about.

I challenge you to spend some time on this. Discover what your sunset is really all about. The truth is in the *future*. For you to be the person that you really want to be, what behaviours do you need to put in place? What habits do you need to adopt?

Pay attention to the patterns of language you use when you speak about the *past*. There is nothing wrong with remembering the good times and analysing past behaviour patterns. However, I challenge you to jump with both feet into a new reality. What is going to work today? What do I need to get rid of from my past? What actions do I need to put into place in my business to be successful moving forward?

Change is happening faster than at any time in history. How exciting to be a part of it!

Quick questions

» What does your 12-month sunset look like for you professionally?

» What actions do you need to take to achieve it?

» How could you get better at living in the now?

» What are the chips on your shoulder that sometimes hold you back? How do they sabotage your success?

» To turn those chips into learning, ask yourself, why do you think those things happened? What did you learn? How does knowing that improve your ability to be successful now?

» Have you idealised the past and the way things used to be in a way that is not constructive?

» Have you felt paralysed in the land in-between, wondering what should be the plan moving forward?

» Do you need to embrace a new reality in your business and adopt some new habits and behaviours?

We can **create** a sunset for ourselves by creating a **perfect** **world** scenario for the future.

_____

SUMMARY OF PART I
Influencing yourself – action and clarity

The first part of this book was about influencing yourself. It was about getting yourself to take action to achieve what it is you are after. I hope you are able to use the tools of breaking down the e-wall, butterfly and sunset to get yourself taking action towards your perfect scenario and gain clarity about the life that you want to live — both professionally and personally.

For more information and a video link to hear me speak about these tools, please visit **www.chrishelder.com.**

Part II
Influencing others: inspiring and motivating

The second part of this book is about genuine communication. I have broken it up into the four communication tools that I use more than any others with my clients and with my friends. When I say that, I mean that I use these tools in everyday life. I use them in meetings, sales calls and parties. They are literally tools that you can use in every context of your life to help you get your own way. They can be used in parenting, relationships and even for—nightclub excellence! Have fun with them. They are so easy to use and think about.

These chapters cover persuasion, conversation and reading different kinds of people.

Here we go! Here are the first three claims on the first three tools presented in this book. They are simply the greatest tool *ever* for creating presence, the greatest tool *ever* for communication and finally, the greatest tool *ever* for persuasion!

Did I oversell that? I don't think so. These tools work. Here they are.

Tool number 4: act as if

- » The keys to improving your body language and increasing your presence.

- » Assessing how you are perceived by others and how you show up every day.

- » Five adjustments that dramatically improve your ability to influence others.

Tool number 5: FOR, ORF, ROF

- » Mastering the art of small talk and conversation.

- » Mastering the art of sales and leadership.

- » Mastering the art of customer management.

Tool number 6: positive, positive, positive – negative

» Understanding how the pleasure–pain principle works.

» Getting others to take action.

» Creating leverage to get clients to make decisions.

Tool number 7: the colours

» How to read the preferences of different types of personalities.

» How to use that information to influence others in sales, leadership and life.

» Understanding the power of timeline and how different types of personalities process information differently.

All of these tools are simple concepts and tools that you can use immediately. They all are fantastic. Enjoy the ride!

CHAPTER 4
Tool number 4: act as if

Albert Mehrabian, Professor Emeritus of Psychology at UCLA, is well known for his study on body language and is often quoted in NLP courses. It said that only 7 per cent of your communication is conveyed by words. This is obviously a very small number. But 38 per cent of your communication is conveyed through the tone in which you say something. That makes tone five times more powerful than the words you use.

There must be some truth in this as experience often shows us that tone is more powerful than words. You know this is true if you've been in a relationship. A man looks at his wife and asks with a confused look on his face, 'Sweetheart, what is the matter? *Is something the matter?* Have I done something? What is *wrong*?'

'*Nothing!* Stop asking me. Nothing is the matter!' she screams.

I hope he doesn't respond by saying, 'Well, that's good. I didn't think there was.'

Of course something is wrong.

Actually, most of us are pretty good at picking up tone and we realise that tone is often more important than words. Most of us are good at picking up things like sarcasm, sincerity and insincerity.

Mehrabian also said that 55 per cent of our communication is conveyed by body language. And while these percentages are some of the most quoted by motivational speakers around the world, a lot of people have also tried to refute the exact numbers. Either way, moving the numbers to the side, there is no doubt that the most important and powerful form of communication is our body language. The actual percentages really are hard to know, but in simple terms, your body language in most situations is your most powerful way to unconsciously influence other people.

Tool number 4, act as if, will challenge you to think about how you show up every day with your most powerful form of communication — your body language. What would other people say about you in terms of how you carry yourself? What would they say about how confident they perceive you to be? How would they describe you when you enter a room? Are you happy about what the answer to that question would be?

The great news is that you can very quickly change how you influence people at an unconscious level. It all starts with three words. These are the greatest three words! These are the three words that fundamentally changed the course of my life as I look back. Those three words are *act as if.*

Let me explain. If you want to be the person that you would really like to be, let me ask you a question — how would *that* person act? Act as if you are that person and act as if you would do the things that they would do. I want you to watch how change starts to take place.

If you were going to be a great leader, how would you *walk*? How would you *hold* yourself, how would you *carry* yourself? What books would you *read*? What would you *think* about? What sort of television shows would you *watch*? What things would you *not* watch? What things would you *not* cloud your mind with if you were going to be an outstanding leader? How do the best leaders *dress*, how do they hold themselves, how do they carry themselves? How do they *move*?

By the same token, if you were going to be a great salesperson, how would you *walk*? How would you *hold* yourself, how would you *carry* yourself? What books would you *read*? What would you *think* about? What sort of television shows would you *watch*? What things would you *not* watch, what things would you *not* cloud your mind with if you were going to be an outstanding salesperson? How do the best salespeople *dress*, how do they hold themselves, how do they carry themselves? How do they *move*?

It is no different with parenting. If you were going to be a great parent, what sort of things would you read, what sort of things would you watch? How do great parents dress? What sort of activities do great parents *do*? Act as if you are that person and change will instantly start to take place. You can have absolutely clarity about who you really want to be and how they would act accordingly.

The question, however, is how do you get started?

Getting started with act as if

I want to share with you a series of simple shifts to get you on the right path. I am going to ask you to hold up a mirror and examine your personal brand and how well you are doing at attracting others. I want you to grade yourself in each of the areas that I am about to share with you. These areas can be improved instantly, so I want you to score yourself on a scale between one and 10 in each of these five key areas:

1. posture
2. eye contact
3. smile

4. gratitude

5. energy.

Let's look at them in detail.

1 POSTURE

How do you move and how do you hold yourself? There is a way that successful people move. There is a way the best leaders sit in meetings and conferences. I see so many young people and the terrible posture that they assume. Consider the advice given to young people, 'Dress for where you're going, not where you are.' I say: 'Posture for where you're going, not for where you are.' Act as if!

Posture yourself in a way that demonstrates that you intend to be successful! I see so many people sitting at the weekly meeting slumped over like they can barely hold themselves upright.

How do you sit in your company meetings? How do you sit in your sales meetings? How do you sit at training sessions? How do you walk into the office first thing in the morning? What posture do you assume when you are about to walk into your house at the end of a hard day? What posture do you take on when you are about to go to the gym and have a workout? What posture do you assume when your kids say they want to show you something?

The mind–body loop is alive and well. If you watch someone with excellent posture, they are alert and awake with their body language. Make no mistake, the mind follows suit. When the body is alert and awake, the mind is alert and awake as well.

Healthy people have better posture than sick people. Happy people have better posture than sad people. Successful people have better posture than people who feel like a complete failure.

Other people respond to posture. Therefore, change your posture and instantly change the way others view you.

Go ahead: score yourself. How good are you at owning a posture for excellence? How do you show up every day with your posture? Give yourself a score between one and 10.

2 EYE CONTACT

Do you believe that eyes are the windows to the soul?

Eyes are amazing. I can be standing on stage and catch someone's eye and I can feel the intensity with which they are listening. I can feel that they are connected to what is being said. Eyes create an instant connection.

Sometimes that connection can be good and sometimes that connection can be bad. You may have had the experience of making a connection with someone that you did not want to connect with. Have you ever been walking down a busy street and caught someone's eyes from 20 metres away? You can tell right away that this person has *crazy eyes*. You're walking along one way and you switch direction instantly! Or, maybe you were driving your car and caught someone's eyes through your windscreen and their windscreen. The contact may only last a second, but there was a connection. It was a quick relationship, but it could be a good one!

One observation that I have made over the years is that the truly great leaders are very good at *looking* at people. They make eye contact and they present an image of a person who is confident and in control of themselves. Most employees want to be inspired by the people they work for. So much of that inspiration comes from feeling a connection with their leader. There is no quicker way to gain a connection than by making eye contact with that employee.

However, I have also observed that many bosses often forget to look at the people they are managing or leading and therefore have a low level of connection with the message they are sending. It is the same with salespeople. It is staggering how many salespeople never really *look* at their clients. The minute that they walked out of the appointment, they would not know the colour of the clients' eyes because they never really looked.

I have spent a great deal of time out on the road with salespeople. I have gone along with salespeople on hundreds of appointments. The first question I ask them when we come out of the appointment is: 'What colour tie was he wearing? What kind of jewellery was she wearing?' Nine times out of 10 the salesperson cannot tell me because they never really *looked*. They were so busy flipping pages through their presentation that they were never really present with the client. They were simply turning pages and the client failed to connect with the message that the salesperson was trying to send.

Many parents do the same thing. The child walks into the room and they say, 'Mum, Dad — look at the picture I drew.' The parent, who is in the middle of any number of a thousand tasks that take up the day of a parent with a young child, never really makes eye contact with the child. Instead, they glance in their direction and respond with a fleeting:

> That's great, sweetie. I'll have a proper look later, but right now I've got to get dinner ready.

They didn't *really* look at the child. They didn't *really* look at the picture. When it really comes down to it, they have missed an opportunity to connect with their child. They had an opportunity to get down on one knee, to the level of the child, look them in the eyes and say, 'That is beautiful, that is fantastic.' They missed the opportunity.

It is the same in a relationship. People forget to make eye contact with the people they love. Their partner walks in and says, 'Hey, honey! How was your day?' How often does it happen that the other person quickly smiles while checking their emails on their phone: 'Good — good. Let me just quickly check my emails and I'll be with you in a minute.'

It happens all the time. When you fail to look, you don't actually connect.

I always tell audiences that next to the words *eye contact*, I want them to write down the words *be present*. When people are present, they naturally look at people.

Now remember, I am not talking about incessantly staring at someone to the extent that you are beginning to freak them out. It is not about big saucer eyes that start to look like crazy eyes! Instead, it is about appropriate eye contact and connection that demonstrate you are present in the conversation you are having.

Maybe when you grew up you had a father or mother who sat at the dinner table and, even though they were physically there, they weren't *really* there. You could ask them a question or even walk up to them and put your arms around them. You could punch them on the shoulder or pour them a drink. Even though they were right in front of you, in reality they were still at work!

Perhaps that still happens to you. Are you *present* at the dinner table? Are you present in the sales meeting? Are you present in the boardroom meeting? There is great power in being able to influence other people when they know someone is listening to them. Everyone has had the experience of talking to someone whose eyes are glazing over in the middle of the conversation. You cannot influence people with glazed eyes.

How *present* are you? How good are you at looking at people and making eye contact that lets them know that you are listening to them and not distracted? Give yourself a score between one and 10 on eye contact. How good are you at looking and being present?

3 SMILE

This is a very simple one. How often do you smile? Some people are smilers. Some people smile all the time. They walk in the office and they're smiling. They sit in a meeting and they're smiling. They go for a performance review and they're smiling. They are good at it!

Some people are the opposite. I often make reference to these people in the conferences I speak at. As I say, 'Most of you are smilers', I say, pointing people out. 'You, sir, are a smiler! You, ma'am, are a smiler! You are definitely a smiler. There are a few of you looking at me right now and saying, "I don't know, Chris. I tried that once and it really didn't work for me!"'

For most people, the place to be is probably somewhere in between smiling all the time and never smiling. The bottom line is that people want to spend more time with others that make them feel good. There is no quicker way to make someone else feel good about themselves than to smile at them. It is also the quickest way to make you feel better. For the purpose of *influence*, I think it worth repeating: the quickest way to make someone feel good about themselves is to smile at them.

How often do you smile? How often do you really smile at someone and make them feel special? Smiling is the quickest way to make someone feel special. How good at it are you? How often do you freely smile? How often do you experience joy? Are you living a life of joy or are you living a life of obligation? What would get you to smile more often? How often do you laugh?

Give yourself a score between one and 10 on how often you influence other people through smiling.

4 GRATITUDE

Gratitude really drives the bus on the first three shifts to make — posture, eye contact, smile. In other words, without gratitude, the other three may feel forced. I like the participants at the conferences that I speak at to have fun and exaggerate the first three shifts. They walk around with exaggerated posture, crazy eyes and toothy smiles. They have fun, but this is obviously not it. This won't influence anybody. The reason for that is that they are coming from the outside in instead of from the inside out. When you drive gratitude from the inside first, the shifts on the outside happen very naturally.

Do you spend the majority of your time focused on what you do have, or do you spend most of the time focused on the things that you don't have? Do you spend enough time appreciating the things you love, or do you spend too much time thinking about the things that are missing? Ultimately, do you spend the majority of your time thinking about the things that are right or do you spend most of your time thinking about the things that are wrong?

Tomorrow morning, when you to wake up, I want you to notice something about yourself. When you first wake up in the morning, I want you to notice what the first seven things you think about are. The most important words of all are the words you say to yourself, about yourself, when you are alone by yourself. What are the first seven things that you say to yourself?

For some people the first seven things they think about are things like, 'Stupid alarm clock!' 'My head!' 'Why did I drink so much last night?' 'I have to stop drinking during the week.' 'It's not my head, it's my back!' Then they turn around and look at their partner lying in bed, still asleep, groan and grumble under their breath and wonder what they ever saw in them in the first place as they stumble into the bathroom. More thoughts then go through their head: 'I wish we lived in a different house.' 'I wish we had enough money to renovate this bathroom.' 'I don't want to take the train!' 'I don't want to take the bus!' 'I wish we had a better car.' 'I don't want to go and fight the traffic!' 'My job sucks!'

Are the first seven things *you* say in the morning negative, or are they positive?

Tip

Consider the things in your life that you are grateful for to focus on to start your day. They might be:

» health

» family

» friends

» job

» opportunities

» experiences

» learning.

One of my favourite words is *trajectory*. I am a huge believer that gratitude drives the trajectory of your day. In other words, when we start the day from a place of gratitude it is much easier to gain momentum to create success. What has been the trajectory of your life over the last 12 months? Is the trajectory up or down? Are you more, or less, connected to your job than you were 12 months ago? Is the trajectory going up or is the trajectory going down? Is your body better or worse than it was 12 months ago? Is the trajectory of health and fitness getting better or is it worse than it was 12 months ago. Is your relationship stronger or weaker than it was 12 months ago? What is the trajectory of your life in these areas? Is it going up or down?

Tip

Gratitude drives trajectory. Notice the quality of your day when you start the day from a place of gratitude. If the most important words you say all day are the words you say to yourself about yourself when you are alone by yourself, when those words are positive, you create a positive trajectory that you can build on throughout the day.

Notice what happens when you start the day from a place of *no* gratitude. If you have said negative things to yourself, your day starts a negative trajectory. You have negative thoughts. That leads you to begin to attract negative people and events. Then it becomes easy to begin attracting negative responses from people.

When you are grateful, the quality of your day goes up. The trajectory goes up. Your posture improves and it becomes easier to look at people and smile.

How good are you at starting every day from a place that drives a positive trajectory? Give yourself a score between one and 10 on your daily level of gratitude.

5 ENERGY

Energy is the fifth part of act as if — posture, eye contact, smile, gratitude, energy — and I believe it is the most important. I say that only because it is virtually impossible to do the other four well without energy in abundance.

> **Tip**
>
> Abundance is a great word. We live in an abundant society today. If you want more out of life, you live in a world where you can go get it! But not many people were raised to understand abundance. I was taught the same thing you probably were. Do you remember this saying: a bird in the hand is better than two in the bush... That was the best advice that you could possibly have been given in 1929! Today, we live in an abundant society. We live in a world of abundance. Take the bird in the hand, go get the two in the bush — and you will have *three*!

The reality is that of all the truly successful people I have had the privilege of meeting and working with, I have never met a truly successful person who did not possess this quality of energy in abundance. They have energy and it is contagious. They have made the *decision* to possess and enjoy boundless energy.

Some of you may have noticed that last sentence: they made a decision to have energy. Most people believe their energy level controls them, instead of the other way around. You are totally and completely in control of the level of energy you have on any given day.

Energy is a decision

I want you to remember that statement. It is one of the absolute keys to influencing others. You can't do it without energy and the good thing is you can have as much energy as you want. You just have to decide to have more. It is there for you in abundance.

But most people are *tired*. If you doubt this, you can walk up to most people on any given day, ask them how they are feeling and they will tell you. Often, the response is simple: 'Oh, man, I'm tired today.' Ask them why: 'I don't know. I got 10 hours sleep last night. I'm just exhausted.' Walk up to a 25-year-old and ask them: 'Yeah (yawn). I'm tired for sure.' Ask them why: 'I don't know. I'm young and I've got my whole life ahead of me, but I'm exhausted.'

Somehow most people have learned to say this. I don't actually believe most of these people are tired. For most people, tired is about disconnect. I believe most people are tired when they are disconnected from their lives, their jobs and their relationships.

Energy is a decision. Because when you do feel connected to your life, you don't feel tired. You have energy! Energy is one of those things that you can just take more of when you decide to be completely connected to your life. You can decide that you need less sleep. You can actually just decide you are a morning person. You can decide that you have energy to work out every day.

I'll prove this to you. I will prove to you that energy is a decision. Imagine a Saturday afternoon — you know, that Saturday afternoon when you are *so* tired. You can barely drag yourself to the couch to watch television and you feel yourself fall into the couch. You want to watch television, only your outstretched hand cannot reach the remote. Never mind, you say, I'll just lie here.'

Then your partner walks in the room having just baked a chocolate cake. 'Honey,' they say, 'would you like a piece of chocolate cake?'

You spring up off the couch and say emphatically, 'Yeah, babe, I'd love one!'

You found energy. You made a decision to have energy. The simple fact is that you connected to the chocolate cake. You will decide to have more energy when you are connected to your life.

Take the energy. It's there for you. You simply cannot maximise your level of success and influence without it. Energy is a decision. Write that down somewhere and remind yourself to stay connected each day. How full of abundant energy are you? Give yourself a score between one and 10 on your daily energy level.

Exercise

I want to challenge you to have a look at your scores in each of the five areas of act as if. Obviously, you will be better naturally at some of these than others. However, I want to ask you to write down the *one* thing that you can do instantly to change a score that needs the most attention. The great thing about act as if is that it only takes a decision and you can make instant change.

Act as if as a management tool

If you are in a management position at work, I want you to consider the greatest leader that you ever worked for. What was it about that person that made people want to follow them? What were the characteristics that made them great? I want you to consider how they approached their posture, eye contact, smile, gratitude and energy level. What did they do to inspire others?

The key is to recognise what great leaders do, and act as if you are leading in the same way they did.

Think of a manager or boss that you had in your life who was a terrible leader of people. Perhaps this person put you down or hurt your feelings in the past. They were a manager who took away your power and you resented their instructions? What were the characteristics of that manager? Consider how that person approached their posture, eye contact, smile, gratitude and energy level. What behaviours of theirs de-motivated others?

Once again, you can use this observation to make sure that these are qualities that you do not want to emulate. Do not act as if you are this person. The interesting thing, however, is that very often managers do demonstrate the same behaviours of the boss that they had when they were starting out. That, by the way, could be a terrible thing. They will be doing the same negative behaviours simply because they are being reactive and it is what they observed from their own experience.

Instead, act as if is about making a conscious decision about the type of manager that you want to be. Consider all of the behaviours you have observed, and act as if you are the leader that inspires others.

Exercise

It is also important to understand what behaviours you want from your team. A great exercise to run with your team is to work out the characteristics of a successful person in your field. For example, if you are a sales manager, it is a terrific activity at a conference to identify the 10 characteristics displayed by the best salespeople at the company or in the industry. The idea is that every salesperson needs to identify which characteristics they have to improve on in order to act as if they are a top salesperson.

After that, get the sales team to narrow that number of characteristics to the most important five. Identify what five non-negotiables that everyone agrees a top salesperson has to possess to change or create a better team culture and get better results.

An example of this could be that the team decides it needs to create a culture of increased energy and urgency in what they do, so they decide that promptness is a characteristic that is non-negotiable. The team agrees that, if they are to act as if they are top salespeople, this year they will be on time for every single meeting.

Perhaps they decide to impose a fine every time someone is late and that money goes into the Christmas party fund. Ultimately, the team has to decide what the act as if characteristics are so that there is buy-in from everyone. Most of the time, it is best to get those non-negotiables from the team themselves. They usually know what they need to do.

Chapter 4 summary

What is the culture of your current organisation? How is your team currently in terms of their posture, eye contact, smiles, gratitude and energy levels? Where would you like to see this culture go? What are the areas that the team most needs to work on?

I always say there are two kinds of offices that I walk into. The first type of office that I walk into I think, 'Wow, I could totally work here. There is vibrancy and energy. You can really tell that the people that work here are dialled in.'

The other kind of office feels very different. I walk in and I can sense the quiet disconnection that permeates the stale air. I feel like walking up to the receptionist and asking, 'What time is the viewing of the body? How did they pass?'

Does your office feel like a beacon of light and energy or does it feel more like a morgue? Now that you have given yourself a score in each of these five categories of act as if, I want you to circle the one, two, three, four or five shifts that need *instant* attention. Within these five areas, you can make change in a moment and instantly you will start the process of acting as if you are the person that you want to become.

Remember, the most important words are the words you say to yourself. In the course of your day ask yourself, 'Is the body language I am displaying right now *useful*? If I was going to be the person that I wanted to be, is this the body language I would be displaying?'

Act as if. These are three great words to anchor your success.

Quick questions

- » What does it mean to act as if?

- » What are the five simple shifts that change how you are perceived?

- » Would it be useful to print out a list of these shifts or have them as your screen saver?

- » Which one of these areas are you naturally good at?

- » Which one of these areas needs the most work from you?

- » How else can you apply the concept of act as if in your business and your life?

Your **body language** in most situations is your most **powerful** way to unconsciously influence other people.

_____

CHAPTER 5
Tool number 5: FOR, ORF, ROF

I am not overselling this tool to say that it is the greatest genuine communication tool *ever*! The reason for that is that I believe it is the cornerstone of building relationships. And while we all recognise the modern business landscape that we live in is based on technology, it is the building of relationships that will, in many cases, separate you from the competition.

It is also important to point out that this particular tool of influence is the cornerstone of building relationships in four key areas of business and life:

» conversation (small talk)

» sales

» management

» customer management.

Let me ask you: have you ever been in one of those situations where you were at a party and you became involved in small talk and the conversation wasn't going very well. You found yourself scrambling for subject matter and, after searching your brain, you settled on riveting conversation topics such as the weather. Everyone has had those uncomfortable conversations. But with tool number 5 at your disposal, that awkward conversation will never happen again!

This is also a fantastic tool to help salespeople gather the critical information about the clients that they need to influence. It is about discovering valuable information about your clients and what is most important to them. In terms of customer management, this is the information that makes sure you are able to build long-term relationships with your clients to drive retention levels with them as well. This is the tool that will give you the information to demonstrate your care factor with the clients of your business and turn them into raving fans.

From a company perspective, this is also a tool for managers to understand what is most important to their employees. It is a tool that will drive up retention levels in organisations and increase staff engagement. Employees want to work for managers who care about them as people.

FOR questions uncover what is most important to people in their lives. Quite simply, it offers a series of questions, depending on context, that people want to discuss because they are the things that mean the most to them.

- » F stands for family.
- » O stands for occupation.
- » R stands for relax.

The power of F-O-R

I want to start with the power of conversation and how you will never again be caught up in an awkward conversation when you are armed with this tool. To demonstrate this, I want you to imagine that you are in family setting. Let's imagine that you are at a family barbecue and you are now in the position to talk with others that you do not know. Most people meet someone new and forget their name within two seconds of meeting them and struggle to know how to control or direct the conversation. That will never happen again once you are a master of FOR!

The F questions

Okay, so you are in a family context, so you are going to start by asking an F (family) question. Ask these questions using the person's name as often as possible to cement the name into your head. F questions may include:

» Hey, nice to meet you X. Which one of these kids running around is yours?

» Fantastic! How many children do you have?

» That's great. Are you both from Melbourne?

» Oh, yeah, X. How long have you been together?

» Terrific, X. Where do you live?

» All right, X, that's a beautiful suburb. Where do the kids go to school?

» Wow. Congratulations, X. What a great family.

Notice that with each F question, you follow up their answer with a positive response. Nice, fantastic, great, yeah, terrific, and wow are all made more powerful if you nod your head to support them. All of these words will reassure the other party that their answers were appropriate. It is very important to note here that it is critical to really listen. Don't just rush from one question to the next. Instead, while it is great to make observations about their answers, be cautious to not start telling them all about *you*.

Remember, most people in a conversation are totally focused on themselves. They love to hear that other people approve of the public self that they brought to that party. Which brings me to the most important point — these are questions about *them*. Do not decide that now is a good time to steal the stage back and start talking at them. Keep going with the questions and simple observations unless you are really asked to expand about something you said. If you are asked, tie your discussion to mutual points and find an opportunity to swing the question back to them. Once you have exhausted the F questions, you are now ready to transition to O.

The O questions

The O stands for occupation. This is where you discover what they do for a job. You want to find out how they might have become involved in their current role and a little bit about where they would like to see their current job take them. O questions might uncover, for instance, that they have their own business. If so these are some O questions to use:

» So, X, what do you do for work?

» That's great that you run your own company. That's a big growth industry too, isn't it?

» Do you enjoy being your own boss?

» That's great, X. What's the greatest challenge in your business?

» You are obviously very driven, X. What's the plan over the next couple of years?

» Are you looking to grow the business and stay in the industry long term?

By the same token, the O questions might uncover that the person works in a corporate setting for a large organisation. If they work for a company, the O questions might include:

» So, X, what work do you do?

» That's great. That's a good company, X. What do you do for them? What is your role there?

» Wow. How is your company going in the current economic climate, X?

» Good for you. Do you see yourself staying with that organisation long term?

The questions may even uncover that they are not working at the moment. The O questions are still *gold*. An example of this may be:

» So, X, what work do you do?

» Fair enough, X. What are you looking to do?

» That's great. I've heard really good things about that industry. What did you do before, X?

» Fantastic. It sounds like you have a great plan, X.

Obviously the O questions could end up focusing on volunteer work, charity work, along with the joys and challenges of raising children full time. Regardless of which path the person goes down, I want to share with you a little gold in the transition from the O questions to the R questions. This is one of the quickest ways to gain rapport in this conversation. It sounds like this: 'Wow — you sound like you are so busy!'

Everyone likes to be told they sound like they are *so* busy! That is because in this society we equate being busy with being successful. Everyone likes to hear how busy they are. It makes people feel important and effective.

I run this with CEOs and ask them about their organisation. As we discuss the challenges and critical decisions that need to be made, I make sure I respond with: 'This is a critical time, X. You are obviously incredibly busy with all the decisions that you have to make.'

They love it!

'Why yes, Chris,' they say as their chest puffs up with pride. 'It is an incredibly busy time.'

I run this with salespeople and ask them about their organisation. As they go through all the appointments and calls they are doing, I make sure they are validated.

> **Wow, Max! You are flat out! You sound like you are incredibly busy!**

Again, they get so excited, and reply, beaming with pride.

> **I am, Chris. I have never been busier.**

They are so happy to be acknowledged for their busyness.

Again, you can also run FOR with unemployed people. Recently, I asked someone what he did and he responded that he was in between opportunities. He proceeded to tell me how busy he was going to networking breakfasts and meeting recruitment companies, and having coffees with different contacts. I said to him: 'Man, it sounds like you are busy! You are really attacking this thing, X. Sounds like you are absolutely going full on. You need a break. What do you do to relax?'

He jumped in: 'I am flat chat, mate. I am so busy. Just as well I've kept playing golf!'

The R questions

The R questions are designed to open conversation up around what they enjoy doing in their free time. The R questions may include:

» You sound busy. What do you like to do to relax, X?

» That is amazing, X. What do you love about it?

» Really? That's fantastic, X. I've always wondered about that.

» That's great. How do find the time to do it, X?

» Well done, X. How often do you get to go there?

In a family context, I am going to ask you questions in exactly that order. F-O-R — I am going to FOR you. In fact, before I walk into that family context I am going to stand outside the front of the house and repeat to myself, FOR! FOR! FOR! But I find that it is better if you say it internally rather than externally!

These are questions of discovery that create rapport. Do not get tied up in selling yourself to them by rambling through your *own* FOR information, but rather ask them about *their* FOR information. Notice their response.

Where to start with FOR

A number of years ago I was asked to be a guest for a radio station that was holding a speed dating event. The idea was that they were going to bring together single women and tradesmen (plumbers, electricians, builders, landscapers), and they would have an opportunity to have a brief conversation to see if they wanted to go out together. The promotion was called Tradies for Ladies.

They brought me in with the idea that I could help the tradies communicate at a higher level to increase the likelihood of the ladies being attracted to them. What we learned very quickly, of course, is that what ladies like about tradies has absolutely *nothing* to do with their communication skills! Instead it has everything to do with the ripped six-pack abs and their tool belt!

Anyway, I was talking on the radio and introducing the tool of FOR. I was explaining how it was a conversation tool that could guide the questions the tradies asked the ladies so they no longer had to think about what question to ask next. The radio host then brought up a great point. Obviously, the tradies don't want to start by asking F questions. They would open up the conversation asking about the lady's family. It would not be appropriate to try to pick someone up and openly discuss the person's family, who they do not know.

It was a good point. If you are a man trying to pick someone up, I don't recommend that you open by asking, 'So, how's your *mum*?' That's just wrong.

Instead, we need to change the F question. It changes from family to friends. Questions might include:

» So, X, who did you come here with tonight?

» Are you roommates, X?

» Did you grow up together?

» How long have you known each other, X?

And away the conversation goes.

In a family or friends context, the tool of FOR questions will guide you straight down the line and you will never have to struggle again.

The power of O-R-F

What if the scenario has neither a family nor a friends context? What order do you put the questions in then? What order do you put them in if it is a business context and you are meeting a client for the first time and wanting to gain rapport with them?

It is very simple. The order changes to ORF. You are going to ORF them.

You begin the conversation from a professional frame and you ask questions about their organisation. These may include:

» Tell me a little bit about your organisation, X.

» X, what are the greatest challenges that the sales team is facing at the moment?

> » How are they currently dealing with those challenges, X?

> » What do you think is the future of your industry?

> » So, X, how are you going to have to adapt to those changes?

You would continue to ask the O questions until you feel that you have an understanding about their organisation and what their role is within that. It is then that you can transition to the R questions.

> » Wow, X, you sound busy! What do you like to do to get away from it all?

> » What do you do to relax, X?

Following a discussion of travel, golf, yoga, football, swimming or running, the next transition is back to the F questions. This could, once again, be family or friends depending on the context.

If there is evidence that they have a family, you may pursue the line of family questioning:

> » I see a ring on your finger, X. You are married? Fantastic. Do you have children?

> » That's great, X! Is that a photo of your children? (In an office setting.)

> » Fantastic. How old are they now, X?

If there is no family evidence, the friends path may be the most appropriate and questions may include:

> » You mentioned before that you are on the board, X. Do you know Steve Y?

> » Wow, X! It is a small world. I have known Steve for years. How did you meet him?

> » You may know Amanda as well. I worked with her in my previous role.

You are now working to connect on a more personal level (either family or friends) and gaining a deeper level of rapport. It is possible, however, that with ORF questioning the F may be inappropriate. You will be able gauge this. With many clients it might take months before it is appropriate to ask and engage around the F questions.

The power of R-O-F

What do you do if the context of the conversation is not family, friends or occupation? What order do you put them in if it is a relaxed context? For example, what order do you put them in if you are at a football club, tennis club or yacht club? The order will then become ROF!

You could start by asking all sorts of questions about their thoughts about the football team, tennis club or yacht club, because that would be the setting of these conversations. The transition from R questions to O questions would simply be, 'By the way, X, what do you do for work?'

The O questions would once again be followed up with that great affirmation of perceived success, 'Wow, X! It sounds like you are really busy.' This would lead to the F questions if it is appropriate. ROF!

> ## Tip
>
> Remember, the key to all of this working is active listening. It is not a job interview. Instead, it is about taking a genuine interest in someone else's life and what is truly important to them. This tool is designed to give you subject matter for your conversation. With active listening, check that you are acting as if you are a great listener. It is important to go back to the key shifts of act as if:
>
> » posture (make sure you are facing them and your body language is interested and responding to what they are saying)
>
> » eye contact (be present and focused — without crazy eyes!)
>
> » smile
>
> » gratitude (the mindset is to be grateful that they feel comfortable enough with you to open up and share this information with you)
>
> » energy (this is critical — make sure you are listening and interested without your eyes glazing over while you wonder who is winning the football game!).

You never have to struggle again! The days of awkward conversations are gone forever! All due to the power of FOR-ing, ORF-ing and ROF-ing! Depending on the context and setting of the conversation, it is easy to ask the questions in the right order of the things that people are most interested in discussing. Once again, do not get caught up in telling people about your FOR. Ask them about their lives. After all, most people's favourite subject for discussion is themselves.

FOR as a leadership tool

Most employees want to be inspired. They are looking to their leaders to create a work environment that is exciting and that they can be proud of. Typically people want to know that their leader is genuinely interested in their lives.

> **Tip**
>
> People don't care how much you *know* until they know how much you *care*.

Have you ever worked at a place where nobody really knew you? Have you ever worked at a place where the opposite was true? Have you worked at a place where the leader was truly interested in your FOR information?

A LEADER'S FOR CHECKLIST

Can you answer the following questions about all of the people that you are supposed to be inspiring every day?

The F information about every person you are responsible for:

» Their name as well the names of their partner, husband or wife.

» The names of their children.

» Their pets (if possible or unique).

» The schools the children attend.

Obviously they work with you, but do you know this about the O:

- » The jobs they do within your organisation.
- » The challenges that they may be facing.
- » The opportunities that are exciting for them.
- » The job of their partner, husband or wife.

The R information from a leadership perspective includes:

- » What do they like to do in their free time?
- » Where do they like to holiday? Is there a holiday house, and so on?
- » What football team do they follow? Is there another sport they watch or play?
- » What other activities or hobbies do they enjoy?

FOR as a database

One other really important use for the tool of FOR is that it is a terrific way to track customer information in your database. For managers and salespeople alike, let me ask you a question: how much FOR information do you actually have about each client? Do you know their family details? Once again, the F information in the database should include:

- » Their name as well as the name of their partner, husband or wife.
- » The names of their children.

» Their pets (if possible or unique).

» The schools the children attend.

The O information in the database should include:

» Their organisation, as well as the organisation of their partner, husband or wife.

» The jobs they do within that organisation.

» The challenges that they may be facing.

» The opportunities that are exciting for them.

The R information in the database should include:

» What they like to do in their free time?

» Where do they like to holiday? Is there a holiday house, and so on?

» What football team do they follow? Is there another sport they watch or play?

» What other activities or hobbies do they enjoy?

Imagine the power of picking up the phone and speaking to a client that you have not spoken to in 12 months and being able to access their FOR information. You never have to struggle to remember the details again! Don't struggle — get the FOR information in the database and you will know the children's names and the client's favourite football team forever.

Chapter 5 summary

I spoke at a conference recently and the managing director of an organisation stood up. As soon as the FOR slide went up on the screen he shot up and said, 'Chris, can I interrupt you?' There were 350 people in the room, but he is the boss so of course I agreed. He proceeded to announce to his entire sales force that he had seen me present the idea of FOR at a conference in Fiji and considered it to be the single greatest tool of communication that he had ever come across. He explained how he used it every day and it had made a phenomenal difference in his successful business conversations.

FOR is a great tool for conversation. Think of all the different areas in which you would be able to FOR, ORF or ROF in small talk. You never have to struggle again!

Challenge yourself if you are in sales and leadership. Do you know the FOR information about your clients? Are you clear about the FOR information about your employees and the people that work within your organisation? Do you know the FOR information about your team?

Finally, FOR is a fantastic tool to manage information about clients that will build relationships over time. Have you earned their trust? When someone shares FOR with you, spend the time to listen, focus and understand exactly what is important to them.

Quick questions

» In which context would you use each of the FOR, ORF and ROF in conversation?

» How can you use FOR as a salesperson in developing relationships?

» How can you use FOR as a leader?

» How would you use FOR in the development of a database?

» How could FOR improve the energy and politics inside an office?

» How are you going to apply the tool of FOR to your business and life?

Building relationships will, in many cases, separate you from the competition.

CHAPTER 6
Tool number 6: positive, positive, positive – negative

The next tool of influence that I want to share with you is my *favourite*. I call this tool the greatest tool of persuasion. It is a tool that gets other people to commit to taking action towards a desired result. It is a language tool that works on the premise of the pleasure–pain principle that everything you do in your life is for one of two reasons:

» to gain pleasure

» to avoid pain — or negative consequences.

It is pretty amazing when you begin the process of workshopping this tool. Every single thing you do every day is for one of these two reasons. Some people go to work because it truly gives them pleasure, while others simply show up in order to pay the rent. Some people love exercise. They wake up in the morning and go for a run, which gets the endorphins going, and they come back energised and excited for the day.

For many other people the only reason they would ever go to the gym is to avoid getting fat. They show up to try to avoid a growing beer gut or dress size.

I am blessed. I love what I do for a living. Getting up on stage and being able to teach people about communication and influence gives me a charge. Recently, there was a $100 million lotto draw. Of course, it is always fun to discuss what you would do with $100 million, and there were plenty of light-hearted conversations in offices around the country that day. People were dreaming of leaving their job forever and never working again.

Even if I had won that money, I would still do what I do. I would still be getting up every day and speaking at conferences and working with sales teams to improve their ability to influence others. Deep down it gives me joy to do what I do.

I always challenge audiences as to whether they are living a life of joy or a life of obligation. It is an interested distinction. What are the things in your life that give you a sense of joy when you do them? For some people, they work all day and when it comes time to leave the office, they drive home excitedly in anticipation of seeing their family. For others, the only reason they go home is that they have nowhere else to go!

It is a great activity to spend time identifying the things in your schedule that actually give you a sense of pleasure. But what are the activities that you do daily which are simply done out of an avoidance of negative consequences or obligation? It does not give me pleasure to pay tax, but I prefer it to prison.

Some people are foodies. They love food. They love cooking, eating at expensive restaurants and talking about food. They get tremendous pleasure from eating. Others eat because they get hungry. They don't necessarily look forward to eating. They simply do it to avoid being hungry.

At conferences, I will often ask the married men to raise their hands. I'll pick one of those men and ask him if I can ask him a personal question. They always reluctantly agree and then I ask the question, 'When is the last time that you bought your wife flowers?' There is always a murmur of laughter and relief from the other married men in the room. Sometimes they say, 'Last week.' Everyone joins in unison for a big 'Aw!' Sometimes they say, 'Mate, I can't remember. It's been years.' Either way, there are only two reasons that men buy their wife flowers. They are either looking to *gain pleasure*, or they are simply out of points and trying to avoid further negativity by digging themselves out of a hole!

Understanding that people take action in their lives for these two reasons — pain or pleasure — how can you use this to your advantage? In selling, there are only two reasons that a customer would buy your product. Either it delivers a solution for them (gain pleasure) or it fills a void and helps them avoid further negativity (avoid pain). People will not buy from you if your product or service does not add to their lives or help them avoid something unwanted that is looming.

Introducing positive, positive, positive — negative

It is the same with influence. The tool that I want to share with you is a language tool that can be used in conversations in many different contexts. I use it every time that I speak with audiences. The tool is called positive, positive, positive — negative. The first part of the tool reinforces three positive messages (gain pleasure) that the other person or audience wants in terms of the momentum they have going. The second part is a call to action that creates negativity if they fail to take advantage of what is in front of them.

This tool is incredibly powerful because it builds the momentum in areas that are important to them and then threatens to take it away. Let me give you some examples to make this come alive for you.

Imagine a scenario where you are a personal trainer who has been working with a client who has lost a significant amount of weight under your supervision. Suddenly, you notice that they may be demonstrating some signs of behaviour that suggests they may be falling back into some of the old traps. Positive, positive, positive — negative is a perfect influence tool to pull out to bring them back into line. It goes a little something like this:

Positive — You have worked incredibly hard in changing the way that your body looks.

Positive — You have increased your fitness and you are living a healthier life than at any other time since you were a child.

Positive — Most importantly, you have changed the way that you feel about yourself when you look in the mirror. You have been so proud of what you have seen.

These are three messages that tap into the identity of the person you are trying to influence. They are the desired results for this person. Then it is time to drop the hammer using the beautiful words 'What would be a shame...'. These are the words that will summon the avoidance of an undesirable consequence to re-direct their behaviour patterns.

Negative — Because what would be a shame, X, what would be a terrible shame would be if you gained this weight back and once again feel the way that caused you all the unhappiness.

'I know,' they will say, 'I've got to make sure I stick to the program.'

As I said, this is something that I use all the time when I am speaking at conferences. Imagine I am speaking at a conference for a sales organisation that has been struggling in the current economic climate. They have been selling a product that is outdated and using a sales process that is largely ineffective.

At the end of my talk, in which I have shared tools of sales and influence for them to be successful, it is time to drop in the positive, positive, positive — negative.

Positive — This is an organisation that has recognised the product challenges of the past and has launched a new product that will give everyone in this room the ability to smash their targets this year.

Positive — This is an organisation that has changed its ineffective sales process to one that is user-friendly and will allow the salespeople in this room to focus on what is most important — getting results!

Positive — In addition to that, I have spent the last hour sharing with you tailored tools of influence which will help you succeed.

Now, I drop the hammer:

Negative — Because what would be a shame, what would be an absolute shame, is if the people in this room don't take advantage of every opportunity you have in front of you, and you have another year like the one you just had.

You can hear salespeople look at the people next to them and say, 'No! I'm not doing another year like this one. This year is going to be good!' The tool has created leverage for them to take action!

WORLD CHAMPIONSHIP WRESTLING

Now, you'll notice that I have used the term 'drop the hammer'. Let me explain a little about this. I call the negative language dropping the hammer because I want to make absolutely clear that this language is not negative and mean, but rather negative in that it is tapping into creating action towards what they want and need. The dropping the hammer bit is really a bit of fun to anchor the message.

When I present this at conferences, I imitate the sounds of *World Championship Wrestling* of my youth. I jump off a chair and pretend to be jumping off the top rope of a wrestling ring. When I jump off the chair and pretend to drop the hammer (elbow) on my opponents, I make the sound 'Wha-poom!'

It is entertaining if nothing else.

Perhaps you can also remember back to your childhood and watching *World Championship Wrestling*, where the wrestler would drop the elbow on their opponent. Wha-poom! Well, you are dropping the hammer in the conversation. You are inciting *action*. You are tapping into both the elements of gaining pleasure and the avoidance of pain or negative consequences. You are doing this to *help* the person take action towards what they want or need. In simple terms, you are influencing them.

Let me give you some more examples.

EXAMPLE 1: REAL ESTATE SALESPERSON TALKING TO A BUYER

The buyer has found their dream home but is reluctant to pull the trigger and make an offer.

Positive — You have been looking on the market for 12 months and you have finally found the home that has everything you want.

Positive — This home has the five bedrooms, the land, the pool and the barbecue area that you have been looking for.

Positive — Even though the price is a little bit of a push, it is still in your price bracket.

Negative — I've got the home open for inspection on Saturday. You have an opportunity today. *What would be a shame*, what would be a real shame is if you didn't capitalise on this tonight and you end up competing with a new buyer on Saturday. Let's do this thing. Let's get this done!

Whaaaa-poom!

EXAMPLE 2: LIFE INSURANCE SALESPERSON TALKING TO A PROSPECTIVE CLIENT

I received a standing ovation from a life insurance conference I spoke at after teaching this tool — they loved it!

Positive — First of all, I want to congratulate you on your beautiful home. You've obviously worked hard to create this life for yourself.

Positive — I also want to congratulate you on your financial situation. You have put yourself in a very strong position.

Positive — Most of all, however, I am pleased that you have taken the steps to protect everything you have worked so hard for by calling us in.

Negative — Because I don't want to be the one to talk about it — however, it is my job. If anything were to happen, God forbid, if anything were to happen — *what would be a shame* is to not be protected and to lose everything that you have spent all these years building up.

Whaaaa-poom!

EXAMPLE 3: CHILD NOT CLEANING THEIR ROOM

Positive — Son, you have invited your friends to the park.

Positive — I know you are looking forward to seeing them.

Positive — The plan is to feed the ducks and get ice-creams.

Negative — What would be a shame would be that, if you didn't clean your room like I asked you to, I had to call and say we can't go.

Whaaaa-poom!

This tool is great for creating action. The negative is creating an undesirable consequence in the future, which motivates an alliance with the positive messages. It's really important that I emphasise that the negative message should not be insulting. It is not intended to hurt anyone.

Instead, the *what would be a shame* is simply challenging the individual or group to realise that failure to act will deliver a negative result. I don't want you to think of it as mean-spirited or manipulative. It is not those things. It is designed to create action and support the desired result.

Let me give you a couple of other examples. Football coaches can use this tool all the time. Imagine a scenario where the team has played a terrific first half. The coach should walk in at halftime and deliver the call to action. It might sound something like this: 'Gentlemen, that was an outstanding first half! We were aggressive, we stuck to the game plan, we controlled the ball and we flat out played with more intensity than they did! Now, gentlemen, I want you to listen very closely. *What would be a shame*, I mean what would be a terrible shame, is if you let up and let these guys back into this game!' Then walk out! Say nothing else! You will see the team come together, 'That's right boys,' they will yell. 'This is our time! Coach is right. We can't let them back into this game. We've got to keep up the intensity!' They will jump all over each other and storm out for the second half.

You may have read the above and have thought to yourself, 'Chris, there are more than three positives in the above example. Is that okay?' Of course! You may use two positives or six! It depends on what you are trying to build up before threatening to have it all taken away.

As a management tool

If you are a leader of people, this is one of the most powerful leadership tools you can possess. Managers are often afraid to compliment employees because there is a fear that flattery will lead to flat performance. This tool is *gold* for managers. You can use it to compliment an employee and still keep them moving in the right direction.

Imagine a scenario where Skippy is the new salesperson at the company and, after four months on the job, young Skippy has his best month ever. The sales manager comes out of the monthly meeting in the boardroom where the bosses have just gone through the monthly numbers and Skippy has surprised everyone with a very good month so early in his career. The boss sees Skippy working at his desk, approaches him and then does something which will derail his positive trajectory. He *compliments* Skippy without using the *what would be a shame*. It sounds something like this: 'Hey, Skippy, I've just come out of the monthly meeting. I wanted to come over and personally congratulate you [positive]. I went through the numbers and you had your best month ever [positive]. In addition, I know you have only been here four months but I've really noticed that you seem to fit in very well here [positive]. Great start!'

Then the manager walks away!

The well-meaning sales manager has left all that positive reinforcement just hanging there. What is Skippy going to do? Is Skippy going to work harder? It is very doubtful. Skippy is going to do what most employees do and take his foot *off* the accelerator. Because Skippy feels that he is ahead on points, you will likely see a drop in his sales performance because Skippy has moved into a comfort zone. It is the sales manager's fault for failing to motivate by dropping the hammer.

Here is how it should have sounded. It starts the same: 'Hey Skippy, I just came out of the monthly meeting. I wanted to come over here and congratulate you [positive]. I went through the numbers and you had your best month ever [positive]. In addition, I know you have only been here four months, but I have really noticed you seem to fit in well with your co-workers [positive]. We've had a lot of people who have had strong starts here at this company. You have a lot of potential. *What would be a shame,* Skippy, is not to continue to improve and put up even bigger numbers next month [negative].'

Whaaaa-poom!

Smile, nod and walk away! Skippy has no choice but to get better! By dropping the hammer we have created leverage for Skippy to continue working hard. The reason that he will do this is the combination of gaining pleasure and avoiding negative consequences. Pain and pleasure are the two motivators to call people to taking action and this tool taps into both of them.

DROPPING THE HAMMER BY EMAIL

While the beginning of this book focused on the reality that email can stall the process of getting a proposal approved by having others hide behind the e-wall, it is also important to understand that the positive, positive, positive — negative tool is also great in the emails that we send.

Imagine a scenario where I need information for a meeting on Friday afternoon. The email might look like this: 'Thanks for your time on Monday. I always enjoy catching up and brainstorming the next steps. I'd like to have time to prepare for Friday. It would be great if I could get all the information by tomorrow. What would be a shame would be if we aren't as prepared as we should be for Friday afternoon. Thanks again!'

Chapter 6 summary

Enjoy the power of this tool. The fact you are reading this book tells me you are the type of person who will give this a try. It also tells me that you are the type of person who wants to improve and strives to continually get better. Clearly, you are a person who wants to improve your influence skills. Congratulations on that! Because *what would be a shame* is if you didn't put this tool in place and create action with your customers, clients and employees.

See how easy it is!

Quick questions

» What are the areas of your life in which you are motivated by the pleasure that the activity gives you? What areas are motivated by an avoidance of negative consequences?

» Are you living a life that is driven primarily by joy or by obligation?

» Why do the words *what would be a shame* create a commitment to *action* from the person you are speaking to?

» Can you come up with three different scenarios in your life in which you could use positive, positive, positive — negative?

People take **action** in their lives for these two reasons — **pain or pleasure** — how can you use this to your **advantage?**

_____

CHAPTER 7
Tool number 7: the colours

Have you ever noticed the extreme difference in the levels of intensity of different types of people?

For example, some people have very high levels of intensity and others have a much lower level of intensity. Tool number 7 is about reading the personality traits that people are demonstrating, and matching that level of intensity through different personality behaviours. People are drawn to other people who are like them. So, this part of the book provides an insight into what motivates the different people in your life.

In regard to using this part of the book, think of business clients that you currently work with and try to match them up to the different personality profiles outlined here. When I did a lot of business coaching early in my career, I would inevitably discover that salespeople would have sales success with people who were like them. In other words, where the products were basically the same, the clients would say yes when they shared a similar personality driver to the salesperson. At the same time, business was missed more often when a client demonstrated a different personality driver.

Obviously, the salespeople were failing to adapt. They were failing to adjust their intensity and personality to the client's. So consider your clients as we take a look at the four different personality profiles.

Also, it is important to understand that, at different times, we are all four of these personality types. What I'm really challenging you to notice with people is what is driving them *most of the time* with the decisions they make. Most people also get along well with certain personalities. These are people who have a similar or complementary behaviour patterns. Most people also have what I call a challenge personality that they find frustrating to deal with. These are the people who have a behaviour pattern that is in contrast to their own approach. Keep an eye out for who you think you get along with best, as well as who are the people who you find frustrating to deal with.

Red personality

The first personality profile is that of the Red personality. These people are driven by results and are focused on power and control. They possess a quality that I call eye intensity, as they often shoot lasers out their eyes. They are very future-driven individuals and want to know if you are with them and a part of their big picture plan.

Let's go back to our timeline from chapter 3 and place the Red personality on it (see figure 7.1).

Past   Now   Future

Red

Figure 7.1: the red personality on the timeline

Red personalities are future driven because they are about the result moving forward. Other personality types plan differently in the timeline. Some focus on the now while others spend a lot of time in the past. The Reds play in the future.

If I am going to sell something to a Red, I am going to play in the future. I'm going to focus on the sunset questions and help the Reds achieve the result they are aiming for.

It is amazing to watch different personality types interact. For example, you might have had a Red parent, and I have people come to me and say, 'Yeah, Chris, my father was a Red, and it took me 20 years to finally summon the courage to confront my Red father about what he did. It took me that long to talk with him about what happened in the past. Of course, the response of the Red parent is simple. 'Son, are you kidding me? You've been hanging on to that for 20 years? Get over it! I know you hang on to things, but my goodness — move on!'

Often the Red won't even remember. It's not where they play. They don't play in the past. They are focused on the future.

Which brings me to the point that, if your boss is Red, I don't recommend that you walk into their office and say, 'Boss, I know I'm supposed to be out there on the phones creating new business — it's just that — well — the thing is I'm feeling really *vulnerable* today. I'm feeling emotional and I think I need a hug.'

I definitely don't recommend it!

The Reds are often in a hurry. They want to get the result quickly, so they can be very impulsive in their decision making. This does make the Reds easy to sell to in terms of quick decisions. I always laugh when a salesperson goes out there with the 20-page proposal the company gave them. Tell me — is the Red ever going to read it? Never. They want a one-page summary page with bullet points.

Tip

If you are working for a Red personality and a problem does occur at the office, they will love it if you attempt to solve it. Do not go into the office and say, 'There is a problem — do you have time to fix it?' Instead, walk into their office and say, 'There was a problem so here is what I decided to do to fix it. I just wanted to make you aware.' They will love it that you took the initiative and will probably throw in a couple of their own ideas as well on how to handle it even better next time.

I love the Red email. You email the Red to coordinate an appointment for next week and you say, 'I'm looking forward to meeting for our 4 pm appointment next Tuesday.' The Red emails you back and it says: '4pm is fine CH'.

They do not use punctuation or complete sentences, and they do not write out their name. They only use initials: 4pm is fine CH — that's it! Of course if you receive a Red email you might think, 'Hmm — that was quite abrupt. I hope I haven't done or said something to offend them. Perhaps I should *call* them to make sure everything is okay.' Don't call them! Send it back the same way it came in: 'See you then AB'.

I received a Red email that was a confirmation of a meeting the other day. This person is so Red they're off the charts, and their response was a simple one-word email that said: 'Fine'

I sent one back. My one-word response was: 'Good'.

The Red personality is about intensity, results, control, power and the *future*. Who do you know at your office that is Red? Are they a colour that you get along well with? Do you have an easy time selling to them or are they a challenge colour for you?

RED PERSONALITY CHARACTERISTICS

» Power driven.

» Future focused, not concerned with the past.

» Results driven.

» Sends abrupt emails.

» Focuses on the end outcome.

» Quick decision making — get to the point!

» They want bullet point summaries.

Yellow personality

Not everyone is living in the future: let me introduce you to the Yellow personality. They are people who are living for *right now* (see figure 7.2)!

Past	Now	Future
	Yellow	*Red*

Figure 7.2: adding the Yellow personality to the timeline

Yellows are the most impulsive people on the planet. They are driven by fun! They want everything to be exciting. They want everything to be filled with energy! They are very visual people, so they like to look at things before they make a decision. They want to look at the picture. And because a picture is worth a thousand words, you are going to get all one thousand of them! The Yellows love to talk.

It is easy to tell the difference between the Reds and Yellows. If you walk up to a Red and say, 'Hey, you look good in that suit

117

today', the Red will look back at you and respond with, 'What the hell do you want?'

If you walk up to a Yellow and say, 'Hey, you look good in that suit today', the Yellow will get excited and respond with, 'Thanks — it's actually a really funny story how I bought this suit!' You're going to get the *long* version of the story!

Tip

The Yellows are the easiest people to manip...sorry, to influence. They're the easiest people to influence because all you have to do is three things: love them, praise them and make it easy for them. They are *affirmation* people. They want feedback. They love approval. They want to be told how well they are doing.

Yellows tend to be enthusiastic, charismatic and optimistic. These people tend to be the ultimate impulse buyers of the world and, if it looks right, they will buy immediately. These are the easiest people to sell to in the short term, but the hardest to keep as long-term clients, as they tend to be fickle and go with how they are feeling at any particular moment.

In sales, these people are also the clients that can really break your heart. Often, when they meet with you, you will find things went so well that you are convinced everything will go forward. You are sure that they are going to buy from you. In fact, when you get back into the car you are tempted to write the sale in your book because you are so confident it will go ahead. Then, when you call them to confirm everything the next day, they have decided to go with someone else. You can't believe it! You got along so well. What went wrong?

The problem was that they saw another salesperson after you and they got along even better with them. These people can easily make the decision to go with the *last* person they met with, provided that they liked them.

To influence the Yellow, make your product fun and easy. Take the difficulty out of it. If you hand these people a 20-page proposal, they won't read it either. Show them the graphs, the brochures, the photos, the pictures and take the risk out of it for them. Most of all, don't bore them. Make your presentations come alive with these people.

I love the Yellow email. It reads like this: 'Hey Chris! — Great to see you yesterday!!! Looking forward to catching up next week at four o'clock!!! Keep up the good work! Have fun at the party on Saturday! It should be great!!! Cheers, Mary ☺ xxoo'.

It is loaded with exclamation points, smiley faces and at the bottom there is exploding stuff going 'Boom! Boom! Boom!'

With the Yellow email, reply the same way it came in. Notice their response when you send back the email with the exclamation points and smiley faces included. They will love it!

The Yellow personality is about fun, energy, impulsive decision making and living in the *now!* Who do you know at your office that is Yellow? Are they a colour that you get along well with? Do you have an easy time selling to them or are they a challenge colour for you?

YELLOW PERSONALITY CHARACTERISTICS

» Living in the Right Now!

» The most impulsive.

» Driven by fun.

» Happy, colourful emails with smiley faces.

» Make decisions quickly related to connection.

» They want visuals — pictures, graphs and video.

» They want to deal with people who are similar to them.

Aqua personality

The third type of personality is what I call the Aqua personality. I call them aqua because they're like water as they go with the flow. These are the most peaceful personalities, although I don't mean that they are sitting around a campfire singing *Kumbaya* and smoking a peace pipe! They are really about non-confrontation. They will avoid confrontation at all costs. These are the nicest people on the planet.

Where the Red is like fire and the Yellow is bright, the Aqua is like water carving out a river. These are the steadiest people. While the Reds and Yellows can have tremendous highs and lows, the Aqua is steady. They like to keep the peace. They don't like to say anything bad about anyone else and they don't like to gossip about other people. Whereas for Yellows, gossip is a sport!

One group in Australia that is very Aqua is what we call the 'solid as she goes' Aussie bloke. They'll say: 'She'll be right, mate.' 'No worries.' 'No drama.' 'All good.' These are the nicest men who value mateship, loyalty and trust above all.

The Aqua gets along with just about everybody. They tend to be independent, adaptable, non-political and good listeners. They go with the flow and tend to have a softer voice and dry humour. They want to be able to get along with all of the other personalities and are most likely to be the chameleon — of all the personality types described here, they are most likely to be able to change their colours to adapt to the environment around them.

This is a critical distinction, as their adaptable nature should not be confused with weakness. The Aqua tends to be better at adapting to the personality of others than the other three personalities and keeping the peace. For example, a Red may struggle dealing with a colleague's vulnerabilities or perceived weakness. A Yellow may have a harder time listening to or working through the details of a project. Other personalities may struggle with letting go and going with the flow when appropriate. But the Aqua is the most easily adaptable in any situation.

When selling your message to the Aqua, you have to recognise that they will hold their cards much closer to their chest than the other personalities. They will also do everything to avoid confrontation because they don't want to hurt your feelings and have an uncomfortable conversation. Therefore, to avoid telling you that you didn't get the job, they may put you off and not return your phone calls because they don't want to say 'no' to you.

Tip

The Aquas do not respond to pressure and generally will not make a favourable decision and go with your idea unless they feel totally comfortable with what is being presented. The worst thing you could do is make an Aqua feel uncomfortable by putting them on the spot to make a decision.

Take note of the types of words they are using. Take your time to make them feel comfortable in your presence. Once these people get on board with you, they are extremely loyal. Treat them well and they will be clients for life.

In terms of the timeline (see figure 7.3, overleaf), the Aquas spend a lot more time focused on the *past*. Often, they still connect with a group of friends they had in high school. A group of Aqua men might have played football together 21 years ago, but they still catch up once a month for a beer at the local pub. Why? They still like to connect with them because, for Aquas, everything is about *trust*. They trust those guys.

Past	Now	Future
Aqua	*Yellow*	*Red*

Figure 7.3: adding the Aqua personality to the timeline

The Aqua email uses words and phrases like feel, adaptive, flexible, more time to make a decision, comfortable to move forward or uncomfortable to make a quick decision. They are usually professional in appearance, but can have a softer tone. Their humour will be drier and they will usually remain non-political and non-confrontational.

Who do you know at your office that is Aqua? Are they a colour that you get along well with? Do you have an easy time selling to them or are they a challenge colour for you?

AQUA PERSONALITY CHARACTERISTICS

» Non-confrontational; often softer in voice.

» Most adaptive and accepting of others.

» Do not make quick decisions and hold cards close to chest.

» Do not typically enjoy high levels of pressure.

» Put a high value on trust.

» Extremely loyal.

» Often will not call back if the answer is no.

Blue personality

The fourth personality is the Blue personality and these people are driven by perfection and process. They tend to have a very systematic approach to what they do and succeed in the corporate world because they have high expectations of themselves and of others, as they do not put up with mistakes. They want polish and professionalism, and tend to be driven to improve themselves.

In sales, your organisation probably has put together proposals and reports to aid in the process of selling. A proposal can be hundreds of pages depending on the organisation. So much work goes into these proposals and reports. The Reds will never read them. They want a one-pager with bullet points. The Yellows will never read them: they want pictures and graphs. The Aquas probably won't read them, as they are busy determining whether they are comfortable with you and trust you.

> **Tip**
>
> The Blues are the only people that are going to read your proposal. At an extreme, these are the people who will also correct it and hand it back to you with the spelling mistakes circled in red ink! For Blues, there is a right way to do it and a wrong way to do it. Make sure the proposal is flawless!

It is amazing how the Blues play in the timeline. Remember, the Reds focus almost exclusively on where they are going in the future. The Yellows are focused on connecting with the present moment. The Aquas are filtering information in terms of trust and loyalty, which usually comes from past events. The Blues run the *entire timeline* (see figure 7.4, overleaf).

Past	Now	Future
Aqua	*Yellow*	*Red*
Blue	*Blue*	*Blue*

Figure 7.4: adding the Blue personality to the timeline

First of all, they consult the past and research what worked and what did not work. Once they've done that, they assess their current situation and what is happening around them. Then, based on the fact that we are drawing information and learning from the past, and the culture is ready for change in the now, they will make plans into the future and decide on what they want to achieve. Let me explain.

Imagine if I had an appointment to sit down with the HR department of one of the major banks in Australia to discuss sales training for their organisation. It's a pretty safe bet that the HR department is going to be Blue. Therefore, it is not a smart decision to assume my two main colours (Red and Yellow) and say something like, 'Hey guys, let me tell you a little bit about my program. It's educational; it's also entertaining. It's a little thing I like to call Edutainment, Baby!'

That is not going to fly with the Blues. Be clear. Instead, my approach is to take them through the entire timeline. Start with the past, then address the current situation and then move forward in setting measurable targets. I might say something like this:

'Sales is a process, and only by recognising and understanding that process are you in a position to move forward. We must be absolutely clear about the programs that you have run in the past. What worked? What did not work?

'Once we've done this, we need to address the current situation. What are the challenges your salespeople are dealing with right now? After we've established that information, we can begin the process of setting some clear and measurable targets moving forward.'

> **It is my job to adapt to people that I want to influence.**

It is my job to adapt to the HR department. Why do I want to do this? I want the client to feel comfortable with the process. Take notice of your clients. Notice the people you're dealing with on a day-to-day basis. Where are they playing in their timeline to make decisions?

I love the Blue email. It is the most formal of the emails:

'Chris, further to our conversation, I've highlighted the eight topics I would like to cover as part of our meeting next week. Also attached is a corporate profile, as well as some map references on how to find our office. I look forward to our meeting with you Tuesday at 4 pm. If you have any difficulty, please do not hesitate to contact my office.

Regards, Mary'

If Mary is in a particularly good mood that day, the end of the Blue email will read: 'Kind Regards, Mary'.

A participant in one of my seminars blurted out in a seminar, 'Chris, is this a 100 per cent accurate personality assessment tool?'

'No,' I smiled. 'But thank you for sharing your personality with all of us.'

BLUE PERSONALITY CHARACTERISTICS

» Driven by process and perfection.

» Systematic approach to success.

» High expectations of themselves and others.

» Play in the entire timeline, from the past through the present into the future.

» Want clear outcomes, objectives and strategy.

» Need to be able to measure results.

» Want polish and professionalism.

Applying the colours

It is critical to understand which types of people make quick decisions to act and which go through a significant process to make a decision. Some impulsive men would go home tonight and declare to their Blue wife, 'That's it! Let's go! Pack the bags. We're going on a holiday tomorrow! We're off to Hawaii! I've booked the tickets!' The men would think they were being romantically impulsive.

The fact is that they have taken a great deal of the fun of the holiday away from her. For her, 50 per cent of the fun is actually *planning* the holiday! Which resort will we stay in? Where will we snorkel? Where will we eat? For the Blue personality, this is half the fun!

THE POWER OF ADAPTING

I want to tell you a quick story about my accountant. When I say the word accountant, what colour is my accountant? What colour pops into your head? Blue. There are no Yellow accountants. There are no accountants jumping up and exclaiming to their client, 'Chris, I decided to do something a bit different this year with your tax return. I decided this year to make it a pop-up book!'

That doesn't happen.

My accountant is also an agent for Australian Football League players — sort of like a Jerry Maguire of the AFL. Every experience I had ever had with him at work had been a fairly Blue experience. Usually, someone would come out to reception where I would be waiting patiently and say to me, 'Peter is ready to see you now.' At which time, I would gather my things and go back for my Blue accountant experience.

A number of years ago, Peter said to me that he was missing some business. He was going out to the bush to rural towns to try to sign young players to manage. He was going out to their homes and sitting down with the parents and he said he was missing business because he was too analytical. That's too Blue in my language.

I invited Peter to come see the seminars that I was running on personality types. He came to four of them. Why four of them? Because he's Blue!

The next time I went to see him in his office, Peter himself came out to greet me.

'Hello, Chris,' he said with an electric smile. 'How are you doing?'

I said, 'Good, Peter. Great to see you.'

He said, 'Come on back to my office. The guys from Red Bull were just in the office for the athletes. Would you like a case of Red Bull?' I accepted as he handed me a case of drinks. 'Here Chris, I just got some mini-footballs from one of the clubs. Take some of these footballs for the kids.'

'Thanks Peter,' I said, excited. 'That's great.'

Then he brought me into his office. This is where he had me. Remembering that I have a good dose of Yellow, he played on my desire for approval. 'Chris, you look really good at the moment. Have you lost some weight? You look really healthy.'

'Thanks Peter,' I lit up. 'Actually mate I think I've gained a little bit lately. I've been travelling a bit ... Anyway, Peter, you seem *really* good. I've never seen you so happy. You've got a spring in your step and you seem great! You seem totally happy!'

Peter shot back: 'No, man, this is killing me! I'm just trying to do what you taught me!'

It worked. He had me. He had me at 'Hello'.

Chapter 7 summary

Everybody is different. Our children are different. Our partners are different. Our bosses are different. Our clients are different. We are all selling all the time. How good are you at influencing the people in every aspect of your life?

The ability to influence is all about our ability to shift positions of perception. Most people are walking around in first position all day. They are focused on what is going on for them. How does this affect them? What about them? Maybe you are married to this person. These are the people that walk into the house at the end of the day and say, 'Sweetheart, let me tell you about my day. And when I'm done telling you about my day, I'll ask you about what you thought about *my* day.'

They are in *first* position. I'm going to challenge you to step into *second* position. Shift positions of perception and realise what is happening for the most important people in your life.

The Red personality is about results and control. They think in terms of the future and want their information in 'bullet points' that help them achieve results. The Yellow personality is about fun and living in the moment. They are incredibly visual, so make sure the information you present is colourful and exciting. The Aqua personality is about loyalty and trust. They are non-confrontational, so make sure the information you present them is easy to understand and absorb. They live more in the past, so understand that they are less likely to want to change. Finally, the Blue personality is about process and perfection. They live in the entire timeline so make sure the information you present makes sense and is logical.

It is a lot of fun to work out the colours of the different people in your life. Enjoy the process of reading the client and understanding what really drives them.

Quick questions

» What are the characteristics of the Red, Yellow, Aqua and Blue personalities?

» Which part of the timeline does each of those colours prefer to play in?

» What adjustments do you need to make to sell to each of the four different colours?

» What do you believe your main two colours are?

» What is your challenge colour? Whom do you struggle to gain connection with?

Keep an eye out for **who** you think you get along with **best**, as well as who are the people **who** you find **frustrating** to deal with.

_____

Influencing others – getting your own way

Part II was about genuine communication. I have broken it up into the three communication tools that you can use with your clients, and with family and friends. They are tools that you can use in every context of your life to help you influence other people. Hopefully, they will help you in areas ranging from parenting and relationships to even nightclub excellence! Have fun with them!

For more information and for a video where I speak about these tools, please follow the link to **www.chrishelder.com**.

Conclusion

I hope that you have enjoyed this book. I challenge you to really think about how to use the tools to improve what it is that *you* want for yourself. Go back through the parts that meant something to you and highlight them. We all need reminders to help us get what we want.

Here is a summary of the tools that you now have on your tool belt. You can pull them out whenever they are appropriate:

1. Breaking down the e-wall
2. The butterfly
3. The sunset
4. Act as if
5. FOR
6. Positive, positive, positive — negative
7. The colours

In the appendix I have included a summary of the quick questions from the end of each chapter to serve as a reminder of how you are tracking. Review them often and think about how you can apply the different tools of influence in what you do on a day-to-day basis.

Working with people is such a thrill. It gives me a tremendous amount of pleasure to watch people increase their level of success, both personally and professionally, by putting these tools into place. I hope that you will pick your favourites and put them into action. To paraphrase Dr Adam Fraser in the foreword of this book, 'We don't have an information problem, we have an implementation problem.' Take action and implement!

Appendix: How are you tracking?

A summary of the quick questions

CHAPTER 1 — TOOL NUMBER 1: BREAKING DOWN THE E-WALL

» Can you do a better job at finding out who all the decision makers are?

» Are you consistent at discovering preferred methods of communication with your customers?

» If so, is the client's preferred method also the most effective?

» Do you lay out a decision timeline with your customers and establish clear expectations?

» Are you in the habit of laying out Next Steps at every contact point in the decision cycle with your clients?

» Do you leave something in the chamber for face-to-face meetings? Do you leave clients with a reason to need to meet with you?

» Are some customers simply wasting your time? Are there clients in your business that are simply taking too much time for no reward?

CHAPTER 2 – TOOL NUMBER 2:
THE BUTTERFLY

» What activities do you procrastinate on that you know should be prioritised?

» Do you catch yourself falling into a negative state when you have failed to prioritise and take action on important tasks?

» How can you change your own language with yourself when you feel the butterfly effect?

» In which areas of your business and life will you be able to apply the butterfly effect?

CHAPTER 3 – TOOL NUMBER 3: THE SUNSET

» What does your 12-month sunset look like for you professionally?

» What actions do you need to take to achieve it?

» How could you get better at living in the now?

» What are the chips on your shoulder that sometimes hold you back? How do they sabotage your success?

» To turn those chips into learning, ask yourself, why do you think those things happened? What did you learn? How does knowing that improve your ability to be successful now?

» Have you idealised the past and the way things used to be in a way that is not constructive?

» Have you felt paralysed in the land in-between, wondering what should be the plan moving forward?

» Do you need to embrace a new reality in your business and adopt some new habits and behaviours?

CHAPTER 4 – TOOL NUMBER 4: ACT AS IF

» What does it mean to act as if?

» What are the five simple shifts that change how you are perceived?

» Would it be useful to print out a list of these shifts or have them as your screen saver?

» Which one of these areas are you naturally good at?

» Which one of these areas needs the most work from you?

» How else can you apply the concept of act as if in your business and your life?

CHAPTER 5 – TOOL NUMBER 5: FOR, ORF, ROF

» In which context would you use each of the FOR, ORF and ROF in conversation?

» How can you use FOR as a salesperson in developing relationships?

» How can you use FOR as a leader?

» How would you use FOR in the development of a database?

» How could FOR improve the energy and politics inside an office?

» How are you going to apply the tool of FOR to your business and life?

CHAPTER 6 – TOOL NUMBER 6: POSITIVE, POSITIVE, POSITIVE – NEGATIVE

» What are the areas of your life in which you are motivated by the pleasure that the activity gives you? What areas are motivated by an avoidance of negative consequences?

» Are you living a life that is driven primarily by joy or by obligation?

» Why do the words *what would be a shame* create a commitment to *action* from the person you are speaking to?

» Can you come up with three different scenarios in your life in which you could use positive, positive, positive — negative?

CHAPTER 7 – TOOL NUMBER 7: THE COLOURS

» What are the characteristics of the Red, Yellow, Aqua and Blue personalities?

» Which part of the timeline does each of those colours prefer to play in?

» What adjustments do you need to make to sell to each of the four different colours?

» What do you believe your main two colours are?

» What is your challenge colour? Whom do you struggle to gain connection with?